The
Interim
Manager

The
Interim
Manager

• • • • •

A new career model for
the experienced manager

DAVID CLUTTERBUCK
AND
DES DEARLOVE

FINANCIAL TIMES
PITMAN PUBLISHING

FINANCIAL TIMES
MANAGEMENT
LONDON • SAN FRANCISCO
KUALA LUMPUR • JOHANNESBURG

Financial Times Management delivers the knowledge,
skills and understanding that enable students,
managers and organisations to achieve their ambitions,
whatever their needs, wherever they are.

London Office:
128 Long Acre, London WC2E 9AN
Tel: +44 (0)171 447 2000
Fax: +44 (0)171 240 5771
Website: www.ftmanagement.com

A Division of Financial Times Professional Limited

First published in Great Britain in 1999

© Financial Times Professional Limited 1999

The right of David Clutterbuck and Des Dearlove to be identified as authors
of this work has been asserted by them in accordance
with the Copyright, Designs and Patents Act 1988.

ISBN 0 273 63293 0

British Library Cataloguing in Publication Data
A CIP catalogue record for this book can be obtained from the British Library.

10 9 8 7 6 5 4 3 2 1

Typeset by Northern Phototypesetting Co. Ltd.
Printed and bound in Great Britain by Biddles Ltd, Guildford & Kings Lynn

The Publishers' policy is to use paper manufactured from sustainable forests.

About the Authors

DAVID CLUTTERBUCK is one of Europe's best-known thinkers and writers on management, and author or co-author of some 35 books including *The Winning Streak, The Power of Empowerment, The Independent Board Director* and *Learning Alliances.* David has led the introduction of innovative concepts such as 360 degree feedback, best practice benchmarking and developmental mentoring. An active entrepreneur, he has founded several successful businesses in communication and management consultancy. One of his enterprises is a virtual company, consisting of writers and academics around the world.

David advises companies in many countries on management issues, ranging from corporate governance and director development to how to establish mentoring programmes for new graduate recruits. He maintains a constant programme of leading-edge research into management issues.

DES DEARLOVE is a management and business journalist. Former editor of *The Times* recruitment pages, he now writes the 'Changing business' column. He also contributes to a variety of other publications, including *TIME* magazine, *Fast Forward* and *Human Resources.*

Des has written and co-written a number of books on management best practice, including *Key Management Decisions* (FT Professional).

Contents

Acknowledgements   xi

Preface *by John Murray*   xiii

Foreword *by David N. James* CBE   xix

Introduction   1

The agile organization   4

Importing knowledge   5

Learning to flex   6

Insourcing   7

Free agents   9

1 What is interim management?   11

The rise of the interim manager   15

The evolution of interim management   20

A strategic resource   23

2 What do interim managers do?   27

Flexible friends   30

Booster rockets   31

Gap management   33

Project management   37

Turnarounds   41

Developing people: the mentoring role   44

The Chief Executive's choice   46

3 Why companies use interim managers   49

Flexible resourcing   52

The business case for interim management   55

Competitive acceleration   57

Value for money   59
Interim vs permanent manager   60
Interim manager vs consultant   62
Interims vs outsourcing   65
Interim manager vs company doctor   68

4   Why do people become interim managers?   71
Flexing not temping   74
The portfolio people   76
The new professionals   79
Ten myths about interim managers   85

5   Who makes a good interim manager?   89
The right stuff of interims   91
What skills are most in demand?   93
Interim managers vs executive temps   95
A special breed   97
Leaders   100
Money in the bank   101
Grey hairs   102
The interim mindset   104
Life after jobs   107

6   Marketing yourself as an interim manager   115
The specialists   117
Why use an intermediary?   123
Choosing and marketing yourself to an
    intermediary   131
What qualities does an intermediary look for?   132
What should you expect from an intermediary?   134

7   The assignment   139
The assignment life cycle   141
Quick wins and hidden heroes   146

Preliminaries: intelligence gathering   147
Phase 1: Getting to know one another   149
Phase 2: Defining objectives   152
Phase 3: Setting milestones   155
Phase 4: Implementation   156
Phase 5: Exit   158

8   The future of interim management   167
The future of careers   169
The interim manager as developer   174
Tomorrow's interim manager   176
Developing tomorrow's interim managers   180
The job-sharing interim   184
The virtual interim   184

Appendix: Interim managers: a breed apart?   189
Further reading   194
Index   195

Acknowledgements

We have been writing about career patterns and the changing nature of work for a number of years. Our interest in interim management grew out of an article that appeared in *The Times* in 1997. It was called 'Yes, work can begin at 40'* and to judge by the letters and telephone calls that followed, it hit a nerve. Many readers, it seemed, were still coming to terms with the 'downsizing' of the early 1990s, and a recession that had left many feeling stranded and utterly helpless. Answering their questions made us aware of just how timely the concept of interim management was and is – both for individuals and organizations.

It isn't a role that will suit everyone. Nor is it some sort of panacea for displaced executives. Far from it. But, it is part of a wider move to more flexible working, an approach which in future should allow the ebb and flow of staffing needs to be managed in a more humane way. It is our sincere hope that, through the effective use of interim management, the distress caused by redundancies on the scale witnessed in recent years can be avoided.

In the course of researching this book, many people took the time to talk to us. We are grateful to them all for their time and interest.

We are also indebted to: John Murray, Richard Foot and Stuart Cain at PA Consulting; and Charles Handy for his vision.

Thanks are also due to our publisher Pradeep Jethi at FT Professional, to Patricia Lotery for her project management skills, and to Stephen Coomber for his research.

David Clutterbuck and Des Dearlove
July 1998

*Dearlove, Des, 'Yes, work can begin at 40', *The Times*, 12 June 1997.

Preface

by John Murray
Head of PA Consulting Group's Interim Management Practice

Like many management handbooks *The Interim Manager* pays homage to a management concept whose time has come. One can argue that the time came for interim management 15 years ago in The Netherlands, or in 1990 when PA entered the UK market or progressively throughout the 1990s, but whenever it was conceived, there is no question that it has now arrived to stay in the corporate lexicon.

We estimate that, in the UK market alone, there are between 2,000 and 3,000 registered senior interim managers and several thousand self-employed management consultants working in a similar capacity. A surprisingly large number of smaller public companies and private companies are also familiar with the concept. This book explores what interim management is, but it is interesting to trace the reasons for its increasing use in recent times. What happened to create the demand which we see so strongly established today?

> *Interim management ... there is no question that it has now arrived to stay in the corporate lexicon.*

In a perfect world, an organization's workload in any given period would be commensurate to the man–hours available to discharge it. But it rarely is. Foreseeable peaks can of course be planned for and many industries employ armies of temporary staff in their high seasons rather than incur fixed costs throughout the year. Nothing new there, nor in the existence of staff agencies to service high staff turnover labour categories such as clerical workers, keyboard operators and accounting staff. But, the 1980s and 1990s witnessed a number of massively significant changes in the business environment, which cumulatively presented top management with major resourcing problems.

Perhaps the first signs that markets were globalizing came in 1973 when rapid crude oil price escalation shocked the Western world. Within a decade the development of the PC had endowed managers with rapidly delivered data on their desk top, enabling them to measure market share and relative performance on a worldwide basis in real time.

The banks and the investment community quickly seized on the technology and suddenly the world had shrunk. The telecommunications industry, which had more or less kept pace technically, was given the keys to undeveloped markets when the British government did the unthinkable and privatized its state-owned telecom business. The utilities followed, as did transportation and even the non-policy parts of central government.

The trend spread worldwide under the brand name of 'Thatcherism'. Meanwhile, UK industry, pressed by price competition from the low labour cost economies of Asia, began to 'downsize' and 'outsource'. Direct insurance and banking spread like wildfire as consumers enthusiastically reached for low cost services. The Internet confirmed that high cost producers of consumer services were dead.

Banks, utilities, local and central government, insurers and myriad service providers all found themselves facing change on a scale and of a seriousness that was unprecedented in the lifetime of their most senior managers, many of whom were relatively inexperienced or had spent their lives in a monopolistic bureaucracy. It was of no help to many companies, especially the banks, to see their best people adopt an aggressive attitude to salaries and bonuses and sell themselves to the highest bidders.

The constant flow of faster, better, more flexible platforms and cleverer, broader, more customized software quickened. Total enterprise systems were developed. To complete the chaos, the millennium bomb was detected, ticking remorselessly in the legacy systems of virtually every organization. The time for interim managers had now arrived.

The conditions described above, themselves, engendered interim managers. Many skilled managing directors, marketing professionals, financial managers, project leaders, operations directors, HR specialists and scientists came tumbling out of the big mergers in manufacturing industry, pharmaceuticals, banks and building societies. More joined them on the market as two recessions led to downsizing and outsourcing, not to mention site closures and disposals.

Another factor was at work too, in the form of a growing enthusiasm for personal freedom. Several of PA's interim managers describe their move into interim as a liberation from the tyranny of corporate life with its politics, culture changes and constant re-organizations. Many individuals, who had self-employment enforced upon them, resolved never again to relinquish their status as independent businessmen and women.

Finally technology worked in favour of self-employment in the 1990s, as redundant managers found that they could equip themselves for as little as £3000 with a home-based or mobile office. The lucky ones were even granted help and coaching in self-employment as part of their severance terms.

So it was that a large body of mainly middle-aged, experienced and well-educated executives began to arrive in the business community, assiduously seeking consultancy assignments within their rapidly assembled network of connections. Fortunately for many, the interim supplier businesses were waiting for them and most independents are now registered with two or more firms such as PA Consulting Group.

We are often asked by aspiring interims what sort of qualities are needed for success. It is a vital question both for the individual and the interim supplier because of those who set off down this road very few succeed. At PA we see several categories of interim manager. The key to them all is to discover the reason for their self-employment and their motivation to work. There are, for example, those who have run companies which they have sold, who do not need to work and who seek interesting situations in which they can return to positions of command and dispense their experience. These are usually confident social animals with exacting criteria for selecting a case for treatment.

> *So it was that a large body of mainly middle-aged, experienced and well-educated executives began to arrive in the business community.*

Then there are those who worked for companies which were merged or collapsed or fell upon hard times, the redundant in other words. Some of these are bold enough and good enough to work as interims and have succeeded. But, there have been many who for personal or domestic reasons were covertly looking for the security of 'a real job' and did not last the course as they lacked commitment. Some are self-employed because it suits them to work part-time or at certain times of the year or up to a certain income level. Others love the constantly changing landscape of people and businesses which this type of work guarantees. Some interim managers are loners who are restless in a corporate environment and leave it because teamwork and consultation do not come naturally to them; they may, however, be particularly suited to performing specialized tasks as an interim, despite these limitations. Some are butterflies by nature who are easily bored by stable conditions and flit on once the exciting change management element is complete. They come in all shapes and sizes!

All of them, however, regardless of their individuality and their specialized know-how must bring to the job a range of attributes. We at PA stipulate that they must be highly skilled project managers, good time-managers, analytical, organized, numerate, flexible in their relationships with others, uninterested in status and power, delivery-focused and on top of their domestic lives. They must also be lucid communicators, since their success will often depend upon the clarity of their decisions. They must be skilled change managers.

Proven interims are highly prized individuals who consistently provide value to companies far in excess of their costs. Partly because of their dedication to results, however, they can suffer from a shortage of time to build a network which assures them of future assignments and this, of course, is one of the roles of the interim supplier. PA and other suppliers invest in the generic promotion of this superbly flexible concept.

The future for interims in the UK looks full of promise. Demand is strong, the concept is growing quickly; there is a likelihood of continued turbulence in the economy, whether recession occurs or not. Regulation, changes in legislation, economic currents, technological innovation, ownership changes, strategic relocations ... all of these carry promise for the interim manager of complex, satisfying and remunerative work up to and beyond the Millennium.

We hope that, in this book, inspiration will be found for many of those managers whose future is uncertain and who retain the energy and sense of urgency which this fascinating work demands.

Foreword

....

by David N. James CBE

Few sectors of modern business practice have changed so radically as interim management during recent years. Gone forever are the days when it was regarded as the unhappy last resort of redundant executives on the one hand and, on the other, as the quick-fix for an employer with an inadequate succession plan.

Today interim management is firmly established as an essential component in the Human Resources director's armoury of responses to a wide variety of problems, whilst also having become an established career option, not just a temporary convenience, for many highly skilled professionals. In effect, both sides of the equation, the interim manager and the employer, have come out of this particular closet and the whole mutual relationship has, as a consequence, become far more satisfactory all round. So, what happened, what changed? The probable answer combines a number of significant factors.

> *Today interim management is firmly established as an essential component in the Human Resources director's armoury of responses to a wide variety of problems.*

Perhaps the first agent for change occurred within the overall structure of trade and industry within the United Kingdom during the past two decades. The rapid shift away from old, established production to new service industries meant that a great many older managers, carrying years of excellent experience became very attractive propositions for the new starts during their formative period. A real match of market supply–demand economics.

Then, there has been a perceptible shift towards a greater mobility of executive management, which has increased the vulnerability of companies to the short-term loss of key skills whilst replacements are found. This has been paralleled by the trend towards earlier retirement dates, which may be great for advancing younger talent but may still mean that good productive years are potentially being lost amongst the most experienced management age-group. Another market demand–supply balance?

Changes in employment law have also provided a new dynamic for the interim management market. As equal opportunities have become the subject of detailed legislation, so have the rights attaching to maternity leave become a major consideration in ensuring continuity of cover for, say, a key female financial or legal executive. What better way to preserve the job for the return of the tried and trusted manager during her months of absence, whilst ensuring orderly continuity of the department, than to bring in an interim manager? Similar considerations will often apply in the case of major illness when there remains a good prospect for the eventual return of a valued manager, or when an executive attends an extended business school course.

In noting these changing attitudes, it is also necessary to identify what interim management is *not* and when it should be avoided. For example, the introduction of an interim can never be the answer for a company that is fundamentally inefficient due either to a faulty executive structure or failings in key posts. There remains only one way to resolve such problems and it is not to palm off the corrective action to a short-term outsider without first addressing the core fault.

It is also very important to understand that interim management will seldom have a role to play in leading or implementing a company rescue; but it may have a major contribution to make in supporting such a strategy. The development and initiative of a rescue is the strict responsibility of the board and cannot be delegated. I have seen numerous cases where a board has fallen into the trap of appointing an interim manager to a crucial role in a crisis as an inadequate half measure instead of properly shouldering their responsibility.

In contrast, an interim appointment can be a very effective means by which to tackle a specific problem, which is outside the immediate and routine skill base of the company concerned. A systems failure perhaps; a need to overhaul the purchasing or treasury function? One is tempted to wonder whether the supply will ever be sufficient to cope with the flood-tide of demand for interim IT managers, which may be triggered by the ramifications of the Millennium Bug.

From the interim management point of view, the current market offers many advantages. Indeed, this marketplace is now so mature that many may choose it as their preferred career path rather than as the traditional stop-gap before resuming permanent employment. This, however, is probably and correctly more appropriate for the more senior mangers with some years of experience to their record.

> *The issue is to identify the appropriate skills and engage them to carry out the direct input*

Also, remember that the key word here is interim *management*, not consultancy. The issue is to identify the appropriate skills and engage them to carry out the direct input – not tell you or your team how to do it. In the ideal relationship, very much the norm rather than the exception now, both employer and manager will reach the conclusion of the assignment with a sense of mutual satisfaction. The employer will have got the job done entirely under his own control on a fully cost-effective basis; the interim manager will have the professional satisfaction of having fulfilled a key function, enjoyed the responsibility placed upon him – and now be looking forward to doing it all over again elsewhere.

The rapidly expanding world of interim management is the province of skilled professionals whose task is project evaluation and the matching of supply and demand. How to address the opportunities and challenges of this market is the subject of this book, which I now commend to you.

Introduction

The agile organization

Importing knowledge

Learning to flex

Insourcing

Free agents

Today, organizations have a wider range of options for sourcing managers than ever before. Along with the traditional alternatives of hiring permanent staff or using external consultants, there is now a middle way, using interim managers.

Interim managers can be described as freelance executives commissioned for short-term assignments to achieve specific objectives.[1] In the US, the terms 'head renting' and 'executive leasing' are also common.

To date, companies have tended to use interims as 'stop-gap' solutions while they find a permanent replacement. They are only now starting to understand the transformational power of interim management. It offers the ideal management resource to create organizations that are both lean enough to compete but also flexible enough to take advantage of new market opportunities

> *Liberation from traditional corporate career structures, allowing executives to become 'free agents'.*

This strikes a chord with many of the challenges that face business in the twenty-first century. In particular, it offers:

- organizational agility
- the opportunity to import intellectual capital.

These opportunities will only be realized, however, if companies grasp two vital lessons. The first is the need to 'flex' their management capacity; the second is the whole issue of insourcing as a concept.

At the same time, these changes are also giving rise to new opportunities for individuals. In particular, they hold out the promise of liberation from traditional corporate career structures, allowing executives to become 'free agents'.

3

THE AGILE ORGANIZATION

The case for corporate agility goes like this. Given the incredible pace of change in today's business environment, it is almost impossible to predict what is round the next corner. Under these circumstances, it is increasingly difficult to maintain the necessary in-house skills base to match the market requirements. It is therefore essential to create organizations that are agile enough to alter their skills mix, capacity and focus at a moment's notice.

Experience in the twentieth century has shown that companies tend to oscillate between too much or too little capacity. Nowhere is this problem more evident than with the management population – something brought into sharp relief by the recent downsizing binge.

> *The unwieldy leviathans of the past will not survive.*

In the future, companies will not be able to carry so much management fat. They will have to travel light. The unwieldy leviathans of the past will not survive. At the same time, they will have to find ways to leverage the intellectual capital they need. They will have to learn to 'flex', growing and shrinking their capacity to meet market demand and to respond to new opportunities and threats. In short, they will need to be more agile than before.

According to management writer Tom Peters: 'Agility is the core competence of the future.'[2] Management academic and author Richard Pascale,[3] too, has written about the factors that allow an organization to rejuvenate itself. He calls these 'the vital signs of agility'.

What will these agile organizations look like? Most influential of all, perhaps, is the writing of management philosopher Charles Handy. Handy's Shamrock Organization[4] describes a type of organizational structure with three parts – or leaves. It is defined as a 'form of organization based around a core of essential executives and workers supported by outside contractors and part-time help'.

This model, and variations of it, are often used to explain the move to outsourcing non-core functions. But, the Shamrock model – and more recently Handy's notion of the Empty Raincoat, a fluid body corporate that can alter its shape and composition to match market requirements – also anticipates the growing importance of interim management.

Handy has written about the tendency for organizations to suffer atrophy. Over time, he says, the emphasis within organizations shifts from outputs to inputs – from doing the right things, to doing things right. (This is also echoed in Pascale's recent work.)

The interim manager, who comes in free from the cultural baggage of the organization, and has a task to perform in a given time period, has much to offer these new agile organizations.

IMPORTING KNOWLEDGE

At the same time, there is a growing recognition of the need for companies to look outside their own borders for new insights and understanding. This means taking a global view of the business they are in, but it also means importing knowledge and understanding into the organization from outside. The use of an interim management represents a potent way to achieve this.

One of the leading advocates of the need for a global outlook is the management guru, Rosabeth Moss Kanter, Professor of Business Administration at Harvard Business School. In her book *World Class*[5] she sets out three criteria for thriving in the global economy:

- Concepts – knowing what the leading edge ideas are.
- Competence – implementation of those ideas to the highest standards.
- Connections – access to a worldwide network of movers and shakers with whom you can exchange information and experiences.

The interim manager can fulfil all of these functions. To date, however, their full potential has not been recognized.

LEARNING TO FLEX

In the past decade, a combination of a protracted recession and increasingly global competition has led to a large number of costly redundancy exercises. As the opportunity for expansion returns and companies find themselves facing skills and staffing shortages, the reaction of some companies seems to be simply to take on more full-time staff, thereby storing up more trouble for later.

They would do well to remember the hardships of recession. Through the downsizing exercises of the past few years, many companies have cut staffing levels down to the bone. They are now struggling to find the resources they need to grow the business. You might say they have cut off their nose to spite their face. But there are reasons why companies behave so inconsistently.

The most significant of these is that the employment arrangements that have grown up over the past century or so are based on an out-dated view of the nature of work. Most contracts of employment are based on the notion of a job as a stable, on-going relationship between an individual and an employer. But, this is no longer the reality of work.

Companies no longer provide 'stable state' employment for all their employees. The pain of the downsizing exercises of recent years should have confirmed this to all of us.

Today, the business environment is changing so rapidly that companies are forced to run just to stand still. In this environment, they can't predict the business they will be in 5 years' time, let alone the skills and staffing levels they will need. Once you accept this simple fact of life, the door is open to new ways of thinking about jobs, careers and staffing.

There is nothing quite like a crisis – or a recession – to challenge the way we think. It is only when they are forced to take drastic action that many people accept that there is something wrong with the current system. Many Western companies have had just such a shock. In recent years they have been forced to slash staffing levels in order to be competitive. (Companies in the East, in Japan and other parts of the Pacific Rim are only now experiencing that shock.)

INSOURCING

Downsizing may have given way to the more politically correct term 'rightsizing', but the meaning is the same – redundancies. Redundancy programmes have blighted business over the past decade, as company after company has been bled to cure the disease of bureaucracy. In many cases, the cure seems worse than the malady.

Redundancies are expensive. They are costly both in terms of bottom-line impact on the business and the toll they take on human lives. Where they have been managed humanely they are even more expensive financially.

There has to be a better way. Interim management is part of that better way. It offers the key to Charles Handy's Empty Raincoat concept. Call it insourcing, if you like – a just-in-time method of accessing management resource.

Unlike consultants, interim managers hold line management responsibility. They represent additional in-house resource. They become part of the company for as long as their assignment lasts. They provide an effective way for organizations to augment the existing skills of their 'core' staff – a just-in-time source of intellectual capital and additional capacity. We call this insourcing.

Interim management provides control without burdening the management structure or adding to fixed staffing costs. Unlike the consultant or freelancer, he or she reports directly to the senior management team (unlike outsourcing, they also ensure that capability remains in-house).

> Unlike consultants, interim managers hold line management responsibility.

For these and other reasons, a growing number of companies are now turning to interim managers to provide the additional resources they need. The experience of recent years makes this all the more timely.

As the demands of global competition intensify, the key to success is agility – the ability to react quickly to opportunities and threats. That requires companies with the ability to change direction at a moment's notice; to acquire new competencies and shed unneeded capacity almost overnight in order to optimize efficiency.

In future, recruitment decisions in particular will require a wider view of the options. This is vital to balance a more humane approach to managing people with the need to ensure that expenditure on severance packages is not allowed to undermine competitiveness. Interim management is one of a range of staffing options that will enable organizations to retain their agility.

FREE AGENTS

So much for its impact on business organizations, but what does all this mean for individuals? Here the news is equally positive. For those with the necessary skills and experience, the growing demand for experienced interim managers is creating a vibrant new market for 40 and 50 something executives.

Many of them are finding that the opportunity to work on short-term interim assignments allows them the flexibility and challenge they crave, while the opportunity to take time off in-between assignments also provides the previously elusive opportunity to pursue other interests as well as a career.

For many of those who have taken the plunge, interim management is already opening up a whole new world of opportunities. For some, interim assignments provide a useful staging post between permanent positions; an opportunity for a time-out from the hustle and bustle of the conventional career ladder.

Displaced executives find it is an ideal way to keep their hand in, while they look for another permanent post. But, others find that once they've tried it, they have no desire to go back to a 'regular job' and choose instead to make a career out of interim assignments.

Today, there is a growing pool of these professional interim managers around the world. They have discovered that interim management provides a lifestyle that suits them. They have become free agents – and they have no intention of going back.

NOTES TO INTRODUCTION

1 McManus, Ian, 'Rent-a-boss', *The Chemical Engineer* , 24 October 1996.

2 1997 seminar in London.

3 Pascale, Richard, Millemum, Mark and Gioja, Linda, *Dinosaurs to Butter-flies: the Quest for Organisational Agility*, 1997.

4 Handy, Charles, *The Age of Unreason*, Century Business Books, London, 1989.

5 Moss Kanter, Rosabeth, *World Class* , Simon and Schuster, 1995.

What is interim management?

The rise of the interim manager

The evolution of interim management

Strategic resource

Interim management is the temporary placement of highly qualified managers with the specific task of ensuring continuity within an organization. It can also be put in place to augment the skills of an existing management team.[1]

IRENE SCHOEMAKERS

It is an odd feature of modern corporate life that companies seem to be shedding experienced managers one minute, and complaining of a shortage of them the next. But the truth is that there is always a shortage of a particular type of hands-on manager: the sort of person who can walk into a situation, rapidly identify what needs to be done, put together a plan and implement it within a given timescale and budget.

These managers have the capacity to overcome unseen obstacles, lift the morale of staff, and sort out internal processes and other day-to-day issues along the way. Where they have a track record of successful business turnarounds or start-ups, they are called trouble shooters or change agents, and are even more valued.

Most chief executives would agree that there are not enough of these managers in any organization. So, if this calibre of manager was available to work on a short-term contract, to step in with just a few days' notice, then as a chief executive you might well think it was a Godsend. If this individual was also prepared to walk away without any fuss (or a large severance pay-off) when the job was completed – and was even prepared to help recruit his own successor – you might think it was too good to be true.

But where would you find such a person? To be effective, he would have to be an experienced line manager. To play a strategic role, he would also need to have held senior management posts – probably, at or just below, board level. He might need specialist knowledge of a key function such as finance or IT; or experience of mergers and acquisition. He would require many of the skills of a management consultant and company doctor combined.

You may think such people don't exist, but they do. They are called interim managers.

What is interim management?

'The interim manager is a newish breed of corporate person, who steps in at short notice, sorting out problems, setting up operations or filling whatever gap has suddenly appeared in the management structure',[2] Margaret Coles wrote in the *Sunday Times*.

In simple terms, interim management is an effective solution to corporate crises and other managerial resourcing issues. It entails hiring a highly qualified, highly experienced, freelance executive and dropping him into a business dilemma, with a specific brief and a limited length of time to implement it.

Irene Schoemakers, who wrote her doctoral thesis on the subject provides a useful definition: 'Interim management is the temporary placement of highly qualified managers with the specific task of ensuring continuity within an organization. It can also be put in place to augment the skills of an existing management team.'[3]

An alternative definition comes from the UK's Association of Temporary & Interim Executive Services. According to ATIES: 'An interim manager is someone who is appointed to a temporary position within the management structure of an enterprise either as a functional manager or director, or to undertake a specific short term project.'

In her recent book book *Strike a New Career Deal* Carole Pemberton explains the rise of interim management as follows: 'An organization seeks help because there are major projects where it does not have sufficient in-house expertise, but where once the change has been introduced, the job can be managed internally. They (the top management team) know that they are getting an individual who has not only done the job before, but will probably have done it for a far larger enterprise.'

In practice, interim management can be almost anything that a senior management figure is likely to have to confront.

Scenarios where an interim manager might be considered could include any of the following:

- implementation of systems, particularly new or updated high-tech installations
- helping companies to take advantage of expansion or new opportunities
- an underperforming company, one in dire need of re-organization, preparing a subsidiary for sale,
- the sudden or unexpected departure or illness of a senior executive.

THE RISE OF THE INTERIM MANAGER

In recent years, a number of high profile cases in the United States and Europe have drawn attention to the concept of interim management. These include the appointment of Steve Jobs at Apple Computers.

One of the original founders of Apple, Jobs, who had been advising the company for some time, was brought in in an attempt to get the business back on track after the early departure of CEO Gil Amelio. A formal announcement from the company in September 1997 said that Jobs had been appointed to the post of 'interim CEO'.

But the move by Apple is just the best-known example of a growing trend in corporate America to use interim managers for key board positions.

> *These include the appointment of Steve Jobs at Apple Computers.*

As a recent article in the *New York Times* explained: 'They go into a company for a short period to fix problems for a daily rate, without all the bells and whistles that accompany so many pay packages. In essence, they like to make changes and move on, rather than manage a stable situation or jockey for position in the hierarchy of a large corporation.'[4]

Such appointments can actually reassure investors. In September 1996, for example, PepsiCo Inc. appointed Karl von der Heyden to be chief financial officer (CFO) and vice chairman for a year. A former chief of RJR Nabisco, von der Heyden's main role at Pepsi was to help chart strategy in the wake of a string of operational problems that had plagued the company and to find a 'world-class' CFO to succeed him. Wall Street clearly approved of the idea; when the announcement was made, Pepsi shares promptly jumped 50 cents to $29.50.

CASE STUDY

Background

At the age of 46, my job as HR Manager at a large consumer goods manufacturers was declared redundant, after 22 years' service. This was in January 1996. Although I had been semi-expecting this, because the US owners had gradually been clearing out long-standing managers, it still came as a shock. I decided to take some time out before starting to job hunt, but still took advantage of the outplacement service paid for by the company.

After about 3 months, in May-ish 1996, I started to apply for jobs. I wanted to stay in Leicester, as I have a nice house there and am settled. My partner works in Birmingham, so I did not want to move away. Over the period May 1996 to April 1997, I applied for about 60 jobs. I was offered a job as an HR consultant, but the office was just outside Brighton, and the job involved travelling all over the UK, so I declined the offer. I was also offered a job as manager of an Employment Agency, which I took. The Agency had recently been purchased, was extremely run down, and the new owner decided to close it within a week of me startng to work there. So I was out of work again. I was also offered a temporary job as a Personnel Officer, but the salary was so low, I decided not to accept. Whilst I was aware that I had been extremely well remunerated previously, I did not want to drop my salary too much – call it a sense of self-worth.

I also investigated self-employment, as a freelance personnel advsior, and was about to embark on this venture, when I had a call from a local employment agency – a small privately owned company I had used a good deal in my previous position, and who had stayed in touch with me during my unemployment. This was April 1997. The agency had been approached to find an interim personnel manager for a local company (4 miles from home). The call was on Wednesday, I attended an interview on Thursday, was offered the job on Friday and started work on Monday, as an Agency Temp, on an hourly rate!

The job

The new company had been demerged from a manufacturing plc in September 1996, and was now in private ownership, backed by a venture capital group. It had been part of the plc for so many years that no one could remember a time when it had not been. Once one of the larger companies in Leicester with over 1500 employees, it now had 450 employees, and had not made a profit for some considerable time. It is an engineering company, manufacturing instruments for the automotive industry and high precision machinery. For the previous 2 or 3 years, HR had been run by an engineer who had no formal HR experience or qualifications. He was transferring back to Operations and the Company was searching for an HR Director. The interim role was for a period of 3 months, to hold the fort until an HR Director could be found.

I took over two administrative staff, who were excellent but not allowed to use their talents to the full, a Personnel Services Manager who had a minimal professional qualification, was long serving and who spent most of her time talking and on admin work, and a Personnel Officer who, until 14 months ago, had been on the shop floor, had been chairman of the union, and who was working towards a professional qualification. They adored the previous HR Director (the engineer), probably because they had been able to run rings round him, and resented me from the start. What fun we had.

The HR dept was typical of other departments within the company – it had been neglected for a long time – the systems and procedures that had been in place had fallen into disrepair. There were no job descriptions, no salary and grading structure, and the supervisors were frightened to discipline anyone. Communication was poor, there was a climate of insecurity, etc. ...

After a month, I arranged to see my boss, the MD, to ask for feedback on how I was doing. This was obviously a novel concept to him, and he replied by telling me that an HR Director had been recruited, to commence on 14 July 1997. I needed to speak to this person, so rang him. He was unaware that I was a temp, so we met for lunch, and he verbally offered me a job – this was before he had actually joined the company. He duly joined in July, realized I had not been joking about the calibre of the departmental staff, and kept me on as a temp while he tried to sort out job roles and responsibilities within the department. I decided to take a long break in September/October, gave notice that I would be leaving, and was offered the job of Training and Development Manager, to commence on my return from holiday. I accepted, and have settled into my new role.

> *Systems and procedures that had been in place had fallen into disrepair.*

The icing on the cake

Although my salary is still not as its previous level, I have better benefits – private healthcare for both myself and my partner, permanent health insurance and enhanced pension. I have recently agreed a reduced hours contract – 75 per cent working time and 75 per cent salary, to give me 15 weeks a year holiday as opposed to 5 weeks – to improve my quality of life.

An article in the *The Times* at around that time, described the use of interim managers at senior levels as 'a burgeoning trend in the US', and observed.[5] 'Temporary work is no longer just for typists. Companies are turning to highly paid, up-market temps with specialist skills to help them out of a hole or take on a particular project.'

Some companies have gone even further. In February 1996, for example, the US greetings card company Gibsons Greetings Inc. fired its chairman and CEO and brought in an entire team of interim managers while it searched for a new CEO.[6] The move followed losses on derivatives investments and an unsuccessful attempt to find a buyer for the business.

Increasingly, too, the concept of the interim manager is not confined to companies. It is used by a growing number of public sector and not-for-profit organizations. It is also used in academia.

In June 1998, for example, the famous American business school MIT (Massachusetts Institute of Technology) Sloan announced that it had appointed an 'interim dean' to take over from Glen Urban when his 5-year stint ended. Richard Schmalensee, who had been deputy dean at the school for 2 years, agreed to take the reins for up to 1 year, while the search for a permanent dean continued.[7]

Outside America, in parts of Europe and Scandinavia, the use of interim managers at senior levels is also growing. In Britain, for example, interim managers have been used in one form or another since the 1980s.

> *It is used by a growing number of public sector and not-for-profit organizations.*

Some people[8] argue that the appointment of Ian McGregor by Margaret Thatcher's government as a *de facto* interim chief executive at British Steel and the National Coal Board was one of the first uses of the interim concept at the top of a major organization. Seen by some as Thatcher's henchman, his role in both cases was to manage the organizations through periods of major change.

More recently, there have been other high profile examples in the private sector. Stuart Rose, for example, was brought in as an interim CEO at the catalogue retailer Argos, with the specific aim of fighting off a hostile bid from Great Universal Stores (GUS). (He left when GUS acquired Argos.)

When Peter Robinson was ousted as chief executive of the Woolwich in 1996, Donald Kirkham, the building society's retired chief, stepped into his old job on an interim basis, pending a new appointment.

More recently, in June 1998, John Hirst, who earned a reputation as a corporate troubleshooter while he was at ICI, was appointed interim CEO of the troubled electronics distributor Premier Farnell,[9] for a 6-month period to allow a permanent replacement to be found

But, these high profile examples are simply the tip of the iceberg. In recent years, a growing number of companies have started using interims in less prominent roles. Many of those who have tried it, too, have become firm converts, something which bodes well for the future of the interim market.

THE EVOLUTION OF INTERIM MANAGEMENT

It is hard to pin-point exactly when the first interim manager emerged. But, most commentators agree that the practice started in The Netherlands in the mid to late-1970s.[10] At that time, it was seen as a way to get around the strict Dutch labour laws, which meant that companies taking on full-time managers incurred substantial additional fixed costs. The opportunity to take on executives on a temporary basis was therefore seen as an ideal way to bring in additional executive resource without the negative effects. (Even today, the roots of the interim concept are still evident in The Netherlands, where there are estimated to be proportionately twice as many interim managers as in the UK.)

> *A growing number of companies have started using interims in less prominent roles.*

By the 1980s, firms specializing in placing interim managers were springing up throughout the Benelux countries and the UK. More recently, interim management has also become well established in parts of Scandinavia.

There are a number of reasons for its rapid spread. In particular, the speed with which an interim manager can be put in place is a key factor. To get to the shortlist stage using a traditional executive search firm, or headhunter, for example, it normally takes between 3 and 4 months, but it can also take a lot longer.

Interim firms have a pool or database of experienced managers from which they can match assignments. As a result, they can often provide a shortlist of suitable candidates within days – sometimes hours of receiving the brief. According to one interim firm, for example, the shortest time it has taken to fill a post is 36 hours.

At the same time, the changing business environment in which companies operate has meant that the wider strategic significance of the interim management concept is also becoming increasingly apparent.

Some commentators have suggested that in the United States, in particular, the increasing use of interims has coincided with other developments. In particular, they point to the use of more flexible working practices and the widespread reliance on temporary, or contract staff, especially among start-up companies in California's Silicon Valley. As an article in the

Financial Times put it: 'these companies often employed a core of essential staff on a permanent basis and made up the rest of their workforce with temporary contractors.'[11]

What is clear is that the interim concept is very much in tune with other employment trends. According to *Fortune Magazine*,[12] for example, one in four Americans is now a member of the contingent workforce – people who are hired for specific purposes on a part-time basis. (The magazine says that, over the past two decades, Fortune 500 industrial companies have eliminated one in every four permanent jobs they once provided.)

Still others regard the emergence of interim management as the practical application of the writings of the management philosopher Charles Handy.

But, whatever its provenance there is little doubt that interim management is a timely addition to the corporate resourcing armoury. Interim managers are ideally matched to the changing business environment companies now face. They offer a potential solution to the greatest blight on corporate life in recent years – that of redundancies.

> *The interim concept is very much in tune with other employment trends.*

The Shamrock Organization

The Shamrock Organization[13] is a term coined by Handy to describe a type of organizational structure with three parts – or leaves. It is defined as a 'form of organization based around a core of essential executives and workers supported by outside contractors and part-time help'.

This model is often used to explain the move to outsourcing non-core functions. In Handy's analogy, the first leaf of the shamrock represents the core staff of the organization. These people are likely to be highly trained professionals who make up the senior management.

The second leaf consists of the contractual fringe – either individuals or other organizations – and may include people who once worked for the organization but now provide it with services. These individuals operate within the broad framework set down by the core but have a high level of discretionary deci-sion making power to complete projects or deliver contacts. This describes the role of the interim manager. (It explains why interim managers are sometimes referred to as 'Handymen'.)

The third leaf includes the flexible labour force. More than simply hired hands, in Handy's model, these workers have to be sufficiently close to the organization to feel a sense of commit-ment which ensures that their work – although part-time or intermittent – is carried out to a high standard.

A STRATEGIC RESOURCE

Today, the use of interim managers – also known as 'flexi-exec-utives', 'portfolio executives' and 'Handymen' (after manage-ment guru Charles Handy, – is rapidly establishing itself as key strategic resource for companies.

In the past decade, the practice has become increasingly com-mon in the US, and parts of Europe especially The Netherlands,

Belgium, Britain and Scandinavia, and is now spreading to other countries including Germany and Australia.

Using contingent workers is not new, of course. Companies have made use of temporary and contract staff, especially in high tech industries such as computing and software design, for many years. What distinguishes the interim manager, however, is the seniority of the individual.

Interim managers are typically senior executives with experience at board level or just below. They are almost always overqualified for the post and will often have tackled a similar assignment elsewhere, at a larger company. It is the breadth of their experience that makes them effective.

'A wise, experienced manager is able to provide added value to the shareholders just by being there, counselling, showing the other executives how to make decisions, doing the risk analysis of everyday life', explains John Murray, head of the interim management practice of PA Consulting Group, one of a number of specialists which provide a service matching interims with client assignments to support this growing market.

> Interim managers are typically senior executives with experience at board level.

'The sum of all his experiences over the last 5 years gives the client company a contemporary injection of management that its in-house managers cannot possibly have. Our interim managers are always bigger than the job so they can give their know-how.'

NOTES TO CHAPTER 1

1 Schoemakers, Irene, 'Executive Interim management: Het bedrijf en die managers in relatie tot de Engelse cultuur, economieen sociale factoren, Rijksuniversiteit te leiden, 1989.

2 Coles, Margaret, 'Call Rent-a-boss for a quick fixer', *Sunday Times,* 18 February 1996.

3 Schoemakers, Irene, 'Executive Interim management: Het bedrijf en die managers in relatie tot de Engelse cultuur, economieen sociale factoren, Rijksuniversiteit te leiden, 1989.

4 'More hired guns wear CEO hats', *New York Times,* 28 June 1998.

5 Brodie, Ian, 'Benefits abound when the boss is just the hired help', *The Times,* 26 September 1996.

6 *Wall Street Journal*, Eastern (Princeton, NJ, Edition), 15 February 1996.

7 News from Campus, *Financial Times,* 15 June 1998.

8 Golzen, Godfrey, *Interim Management*, Kogan Page, 1992.

9 Doward, Jamie, 'Problem solver turns his hand to marriage guidance', Mammon, *Observer,* 21 June 1998.

10 In his 1992 book *Interim Management*, Godfrey Golzen puts the actual year that interim management started as 1978.

11 Donkin, Richard, 'The permanent temp is a Handyman', *Financial Times,* 16 March 1994.

12 Cited by Klein, Marcia, 'Sheltered jobs giving way to contract work at all levels', *Sunday Times,* 1996.

13 Handy, Charles, *The Age of Unreason*, Century Business Books, London, 1989.

2

What do interim managers do?

Flexible friends

Booster rockets

Gap management

Project management

Turnarounds

Developing people: the mentoring role

The Chief Executive's choice

The problem is that not many people know what interim managers do. They are high-class temps with a wealth of business experience, of mature years (as opposed to wet-behind-the-ears consultants), carrying no overheads as they work for themselves and prepared to roll up their sleeves and do a job rather than just advise.

ALISON EADIE, *Daily Telegraph*

Interim Managers were originally seen as stop-gaps. They were 'emergency managers', typically brought in at short notice to plug a hole that had unexpectedly appeared in the management structure. In effect, the interim manager was seen simply as someone who stood in while a permanent replacement was found. This perception was often reinforced by clichés that were applied to the role such as 'holding the fort' and 'keeping the seat warm'.

> Expected to do much more than just keep the seat warm.

Although this limiting notion of interim management persists in some quarters, there is a growing awareness that interim managers can also play a much more dynamic role. Indeed, even in situations where they are brought in to fill a gap, they are now typically expected to do much more than just keep the seat warm. For example, an interim can improve systems, adding value to the client processes while a full-time replacement is found.

But rather than simply providing a quick fix in a crisis, today, interim managers are also increasingly being used as a strategic resource to manage a wide variety of challenging business situations. The range of interim assignments, for example, includes:

- turnarounds
- start-ups
- close downs
- acquisitions and mergers
- defending against hostile bids
- IT projects
- rationalization and restructuring initiatives
- succession planning – mentoring and coaching future senior executives

- preparing for flotation or rights issue
- opening an overseas office.

FLEXIBLE FRIENDS

Valued by business for offering a flexible solution, most of the organizations seeking this management expertise have tended to be in the £10 million to £200 million turnover range (often divisions of large operations). However, the range of organizations which use interim managers appears to be expanding. Today, there is evidence that their use is spreading to companies of all sizes operating across a wide range of sectors.

In particular, the interim concept has a great deal to offer small and medium-sized enterprises (SME). Its use by family firms – to inject some professional management expertise without upsetting the family succession plan – can be especially effective.

According to the UK interim management specialist GMS, many smaller firms have a need for a top level input, but only on an intermittent basis. For them, an interim manager is often the ideal solution.

CASE STUDY

The family business

A firm of chartered accountants found itself in a testing situation with one of its family-owned corporate clients. On the surface, the company had mounting stock levels and a rising bank overdraft; beneath the surface were tensions, differing views on strategy and deteriorating drive and leadership within the company.

The answer was provided by the UK interim management specialist GMS from its office in Bristol. The proposal was to identify a suitable executive with a background in the industry and with proven general management skills to move the company through its diffi-culties towards what was regarded as its rightful level of profitabil-ity. The executive also needed to be personally acceptable to all members of the family.

One year later, the interim manager selected had restored the company to target profit levels. He had reduced stocks dramatically and turned an overdraft into a credit balance. Additionally, the com-pany's product quality – a key part of its continuing success – was actually improved.

Until quite recently, however, interim managers were generally not to be found among the financial communities of Wall Street and the City of London. According to PA Consulting Group, that is now changing, certainly in London's Square Mile.

In the past, says PA Consulting's Group's Stuart Cain, City firms preferred management consultants, but today, with a spate of mergers and takeovers and the rush to introduce new technology, the financial community is a prime target for inter-ims. The speed with which they can be deployed and become operational, in particular, makes them an ideal resource.

'The City is obviously seeing great changes at the moment, with takeovers and people leaving', says Cain, who has pro-vided the likes of Lehman Brothers with interims. 'Banks and other institutions have found that searches take ages and in-house people cannot be wrenched from their current jobs to fill in for others. Bringing in an interim means introducing a very skilled person almost immediately.'[1]

BOOSTER ROCKETS

As the number of organizations that regularly use interim man-agers increases, so too does the range of situations they are brought in to manage. There is a growing awareness that interim managers offer additional strategic options, providing companies with a low risk way of tapping into specialist skills for a short period that can transform their competitive position.

> Bringing in an interim means introducing a very skilled person almost immediately.

One way to think about interim managers is as booster rockets. They provide additional thrust to take the organization into a new orbit, then once their task is completed they drop away. Increasingly, they are being used proactively – to grow the business, or implement a key project – rather than reactively – to fill in until someone permanent can be appointed. This bodes well for the future.

In some cases, too, they provide an ideal way to a explore a new opportunity without all the overheads associated with a full-blown entry into a new market. As the changing political climate in South Africa has paved the way for trade with the major developed economies, for example, interim managers have provided a useful way to get people on the ground quickly.

'We are finding that companies are shrinking to their core competencies and using contingent methods, like temps, out-sourcing, employee leasing, consulting services and interim managers', says Ed Steins, managing director of AXIS Interim Management, part of the Renwick Group.

According to Steins, one of the major problems cited by multinationals setting up operations in South Africa is the shortage of suitably qualified staff. In particular, a lot of companies coming to South Africa need a specialist manager for a limited period to help establish the firm or to assist in training a permanent placement.

'We have a network of up to 1000 managers we can call on in South Africa to cover virtually every area of specialization', says Steins. 'They tend to be quite seasoned and are used to achieving the results demanded of senior positions.'

ATIES (the Association of Temporary & Interim Executive Services)[2] says the range of assignments that interims are used for is increasingly wide, but most fall into one of three categories:

- Gap management
- Project management
- Turnarounds/recovery situations.

To these, we would add another important area:

- Developing people.

(This one has yet to be widely recognized by companies, but we believe that interim managers will play an increasingly important role in both the transfer of best practice and in management development in future. The coaching or mentoring role enables interim managers to pass on their own skills and experiences to permanent staff.)

GAP MANAGEMENT

An interim manager may be brought in to plug a gap that has suddenly opened in the management structure. This is the more traditional role of interim managers. Alternatively, they can be used to cover for a senior manager taking a career break or during a prolonged illness.

Typical situations include:

- sudden loss of a senior executive through resignation, sickness or death
- dismissals, both planned and unplanned
- protracted recruitment difficulties caused by scarcity or unusual market factors
- maternity leave cover
- sabbatical leave cover.

As ATIES points out: 'Interim managers will always come into their own in a time of crisis. Companies can often find that they may have been concentrating more on the emergency of a resignation, dismissal, or on the inability to recruit, than on the aftermath and the effect this has on morale and the team which is now leaderless.'

Today, such crises are likely to be all the more damaging because companies have stripped out excess managerial capacity. Managers now have much longer reporting spans, with more responsibility and often greater work loads. As a result, most organizations no longer have any spare resource to cover while they recruit someone permanent to fill the gap.

In the past, the traditional response to such situations was to use an executive search firm – headhunter – to find a permanent replacement. However, executive search typically takes between 3 and 6 months to provide a shortlist of suitable candidates.

> *Interim managers will always come into their own in a crisis.*

Few companies can afford to allow a department or project to drift for that long.

Interims provide an ideal solution. They can step into the breach at short notice; can maintain momentum while the recruitment process runs its course. They can even play an active part, interviewing candidates and drawing up a shortlist.

As John Hird, managing director of Albermarle Interim management observes: 'Companies are so slimmed down now that, if someone needs to be replaced with little notice or a project needs managing, interim management can represent the easiest solution'.

As career structures become more fluid, too, high calibre managers will increasingly demand more flexible treatment from their employers. In particular, it will be essential to provide career breaks in order to retain women (and possibly men) who take time off to have a family. According to ATIES, covering maternity leave is one of the fastest growing areas of interim management.

At the same time, research by the American think tank Rainmaker Inc. and others suggests that, in future, other sorts of career breaks will also become more widespread, including sabbaticals and time in full-time education.[3] All of these developments point to a growing market for interims.

CASE STUDY

An interim solution for IT at BAA, Heathrow

As the world's largest commercial operator of airports, British Airports Authority plc is no stranger to change. The company's seven UK airports are among the busiest in the world, handling a record total of 98 million passengers during the 1996/97 year. All this growth and change requires a support infrastructure which is both efficient and sufficiently flexible to adapt as the company develops. Inevitably, technology plays a key role in this.

In 1997, BAA Heathrow was temporarily without a manager of IT for its MIS (Management Information Systems) department. To ensure continuity and the right level of support for the teams involved until the new IT manager arrived, the company asked PA Consulting Group's Interim Management Practice to provide an individual capable of managing the MIS area and overseeing on-going projects.

The challenge facing BAA Heathrow's IT division was to obtain the appropriate mix of project management and general management skills. Not only were these skills difficult to define in terms of a job description, but they were in short supply in the IT market.

Two issues needed urgent attention. First, BAA Heathrow wanted an independent and objective overview regarding the implications of amalgamating two interdependent teams of people – engineering systems and Management Information Systems (MIS).

Second, they needed someone capable of managing the MIS area during a period of investment, until the new IT manager arrived. The company also required that the individual play a role in shaping the new IT management team following the new IT manager's arrival and gradually transfer responsibility to managers within the new structure.

A sound knowledge of IT systems, together with a keen understanding of management issues was called for, combined with a degree of tact and diplomacy which is inevitably required when dealing with any internal restructuring.

As a senior IT manager with 25 years' experience in some of the largest companies in the UK and Europe, Kevin Lake was chosen by BAA for the assignment.

The MIS team was already engaged in a major programme, as part of a group-wide investment, to upgrade the technical operating environment. 'Project Desktop' involved the upgrade of some 2000 PCs throughout Heathrow, combined with the replacement and rationalization of computer servers and printing facilities in support of the business.

The project, which represented a major investment for BAA across its seven UK locations, moved technology forward by establishing an NT-based server platform and a standard workstation environment, airport-wide, running under Windows '95.

A 1-month review of the two systems' areas to be amalgamated was conducted. The strategy behind the change was to introduce a single source of leadership and effective communication between the two areas which were operationally dependent on each other. (Engineering systems is responsible for areas such as airfield ground lighting and information display systems, while the MIS group runs the IT help desk and is responsible for other management and administration systems such as procurement.)

Following on from this, the overall management and continuity of a 20-person team was required, the management of the infrastructure team and the IT help desk.

Kevin Lake explains: 'The main challenge facing the IT team at

Heathrow is the complexity of infrastructure in cabling and communications, both above and below ground in the 9 square miles of individual buildings, connecting walkways and tarmac. I was given the space to manage the projects, which meant that the new IT manager, from Copenhagen Airport, could walk into an environment which had benefited from the continuity of interim management.'

Adds John Tangaa, IT director, Heathrow Airport Limited: 'Using an interim manager to bridge the gap helped us enormously. Kevin was able to operate in all areas with minimum direction and therefore make an immediate contribution. He produced a documented overview of the amalgamation of the two teams which was objective and impartial. No time was lost while we awaited our new manager and having an outsider on a short-term contract provided us with the impartial help we needed.'

PROJECT MANAGEMENT

The project-oriented interim assignment has become more important in recent years. In part, this is a natural consequence of the lean organizational structures that have emerged from the recession of the early 1990s. The process of delayering and downsizing has left little spare management capacity to head up projects.

Past recoveries have seen companies take on additional full-time managers to handle what is often a temporary spurt of growth activity. The recent spate of redundancies suggests that the boom bust economic cycle has also fuelled a hiring, firing cycle. The costs – both financial and human – have been horrendous.

What 'smart organizations' are now realizing is that interim managers provide a much more flexible resource, enabling them to have instant access to experienced senior management capacity, without the downside. In many cases, too, it is possible to find an interim manager whose experience includes the successful implementation of one or more similar projects at other companies.

> *Interim managers provide a much more flexible resource.*

For all of these reasons, a growing number of companies are now turning to interims to manage time-specific projects. These include the following situations:

- acquisition or sudden take-over creates short-term needs
- relocation, expansion or consolidation of facilities (office or manufacturing)
- company subsidiary or division – start-up, or close-down
- efficiency, productivity or profitability improvement needs
- privatization
- functional projects – quality assurance, business process re-engineering, information technology, finance, manufacturing, logistics, personnel and training, new product launches, franchising and licensing agreements, export development, sales improvement, critical commercial negotiations
- major change programmes.

The transitional nature of projects also means that there is finite objective involved – for example, implementing an IT project, acquisition or disposal of a company. This makes the case for using an interim all the more persuasive.

The alternative in many cases is to take a manager onto the pay-roll with the potential cost of a severance package at the end. The high costs involved mean that many companies currently prefer to go down the outsourcing route – using an external firm to provide IT expertise on a contract basis. However, research has shown that many attempts at outsourcing, especially with IT, involve signing long-term contracts that are disadvantageous to the client.[4]

What an interim manager can also bring to bear is objectivity. Unlike insiders who have been part of a company's culture for many years, the interim brings a fresh pair of eyes – and ears. Unblinkered by previous decisions and cultural assumptions, they are able to make a realistic assessment of the options. Because they are outside the politics, historical baggage and internal machinations of the succession process, they are also well placed to implement the best solution.

Typical projects include managing acquisitions, merger and demerger situations, and helping organizations through other important transitions where experience is at a premium.

Interims are increasingly in demand for acquisition and merger activity. In a recent article in *The Dealmaker's Journal*,[5] David L. Thorpe, president of the US interim firm IMCOR, notes: 'Interim managers are flexible experts who have become invaluable resources to financiers and corporate M&A (mergers and acquisitions) professionals.'

'LBO [Leveraged Buy-Out] firms find they can use interim and project managers discretely through every phase of the acquisition or buy-out cycle to help with due diligence or market feasibility studies, turn around ailing operations, resolve post-merger or acquisition integration projects, implement roll-up strategies, and help devise and execute exit mechanisms.'

> *The interim brings a fresh pair of eyes – and ears.*

The fact that the interim is not part of the company's old culture can also provide an important advantage over an internal appointee. This can be especially important for corporate transformation initiatives.

Managing change is one of the greatest challenges facing companies today. Recent research, from Business Intelligence, for example, suggest that seven out of ten change programmes are destined to fail. Underestimating the impact on individuals and not securing the commitment of middle managers are amongst the reasons cited.

It is now widely recognized that change management requires a special set of skills and behaviours, and individuals possessing them are often referred to as 'change agents' or 'catalysts'. Bringing in an interim manager with experience in leading other change initiatives is often one of the most effective ways to create the environment for change.

Where a particularly sensitive or tough task has to be performed, such as the close-down of a site or business unit, an interim often provides the best solution. Such situations require particularly high levels of professionalism and are often better – and more humanely – handled

> The interim is also managing his own obsolescence.

by an outsider. The fact that the interim is also managing his own obsolescence is a useful factor.

In future, as companies move away from 'steady-state' operations to become more and more project-based, this aspect of the interim management role is likely to become even more important.

CASE STUDY

National Lottery Charities Board

Established as a new operation, when the National Lottery Charities Board was first set up in the UK, very few permanent staff were appointed. Some posts were filled by secondment from other organizations, while others were filled by consultants. When the first round of grant applications was launched, it was decided to appoint an interim manager to organize the first tranche of applications.

An experienced interim was found through the interim specialist Albermarle, ensuring that the Board was able to launch its first tranche on time. The valuable experience gained refined the process for the second tranche.

CASE STUDY

Norwich Union

In 1997, Norwich Union, the UK's second largest insurance group, was going through a major change, in the run-up to its change of status – from a mutual society – and flotation on the stock market. It was essential that the supply of information within the group be guaranteed – 'on time and accurate'. There was some doubt that this was being achieved at the company.

The company decided to bring in an IT director to ensure that the information flow was up to the standards that would be required in future. The job could not be advertised as permanent, however, due to the complexity and uncertainty of the challenges that it faced. Norwich Union opted for the interim route, and, through the interim firm, Albermarle, brought in an experienced interim IT director who took full responsibility for the information supply across the entire group.

TURNAROUNDS

The third area where interim managers are regularly used involves turnaround or recovery situations. This is very much the trouble-shooter role. In these cases, an interim is brought in to fix something that's broken. The individual concerned will usually have an impressive track record of turning situations around. What the client organization is getting, in effect, is a 'turnaround artist' or company doctor.

In recent years, the use of company doctors has become much more commonplace, as companies – not to mention shareholders and market analysts – recognize that special skills are often required in recovery situations.

> *An interim is brought in to fix something that's broken.*

41

According to PA's Stuart Cain: 'A company doctor is a specific version of interim management in a loss-making situation. It's part of the same family.'

David James, one of Britain's best-known company doctors, does not see interim management as the best way to lead the rescue of an entire company, but believes interims can play an important supporting role. 'It is very important to understand that interim management will seldom have a role to play in leading or implementing a company rescue; but it may have a major contribution to make in supporting such a strategy.

'The development and initiative of a rescue is the strict responsibility of the board and cannot be delegated. I have seen numerous cases where a board has fallen into the trap of appointing an interim manager to a crucial role in a crisis as an inadequate half measure instead of properly shouldering their responsibility.'

However, there have been situations where an entire senior management team has been replaced by a team of interim managers brought in to stabilize a situation. The US greetings card company, Gibsons Greetings Inc., mentioned in the previous chapter, is a case in point. The company fired its chairman and CEO, and brought in an team of interim managers, while it searched for a new CEO.

In other situations, interim managers have been used in an attempt to reverse the declining fortunes of a company. At the computer company Apple, for example, the decision to appoint Steve Jobs as interim CEO was an attempt to reverse the losses and restore the computer icon to its former glory.

There are many other situations, however, that stop short of a full company rescue and where an interim – or more than one interim – can affect a speedy turnaround in an organization's fortunes. These could include loss-making subsidiaries, offices or factories; inefficient or demoralized functional departments;

or projects which have gone off the rails and are in danger of damaging the company's competitive position.

Frequently, in such situations, ATIES says: 'The answer is the deployment of an interim manager who can objectively examine and manage the changes needed to turn the company around; to bring innovative and dynamic solutions to the problems and opportunities arrayed. Someone who has no political axe to grind, can't afford to fail, is focused solely on the achievement of the agreed task and who is motivated only to deliver the required result within budget and cost.'

This may be a situation involving a turnaround of a:

- company
- division
- subsidiary
- functional department
- project.

CASE STUDY

Charlie Farrell has more than 30 years' experience in management. He now works as an interim manager, specializing in corporate turn-arounds.

In the early 1990s he answered the call from Tropitone Furniture,[6] a troubled California furniture manufacturer, for an interim CEO. Drastic surgery was required. Farrell managed to save the company by slashing its inventory levels, dramatically improving delivery times, and laying off a quarter of the workforce.

His original mission accomplished, he then arranged his own exit by recruiting a permanent CEO to replace him. The Tropitone board was so impressed that it asked him to stay on as non-executive chairman. Not bad for a man in his sixties, who would probably be considered too old to get a job in traditional career terms.

It took Farrell 30 months to effect the turnaround at Tropitone.

Since then, he has worked on interim assignments as a trouble-shooter for two other US companies on the brink of foreclosure, each worth around $50 million. He claims to have an intuitive sense of sizing up a problem and then deciding how to modernize operations, sales, marketing and finance.

'It's called crisis management', he says, 'and when the crisis is over, I leave.'

DEVELOPING PEOPLE: THE MENTORING ROLE

Some of the more subtle nuances of the interim manager role are only now being fully recognized. In particular, Human Resources professionals are waking up to the developmental dimension. Some companies explicitly state that part of the interim manager's brief should be to use his or her experience to 'mentor' more junior managers.

The American interim firm, IMCOR, for example, reports that a division of a multi-billion dollar machinery and defence products manufacturer in the US recently used interim management to 'advise, train, and mentor employees in technical and non-technical human resources areas'.

According to PA Consulting's Stuart Cain, one of benefits of using an interim manager is that it provides an opportunity to bring in an experienced outsider who does not pose a threat to the promotion prospects of others.

'The interim manager won't upset the succession plan', says Cain. 'That's very important in sensitive situations. It can be stated explicitly that the interim will coach people while there. Often, the mentoring role is a stated objective. One building society client said we want a project director but we want him to train our project managers to perform the role in future.

'That's always part of the assignment even if clients don't realize it. One of the greatest joys of line management is bringing people on. One of my best feelings from interim management is that the people I put in place are still there and doing well. I get a real buzz from that. That's true of many interim managers. Developing middle management is where they get their buzz – the people side.'

There are two important dimensions to this:

- transfer of best practice and specific knowledge
- coaching in general management skills.

The first of these is when the interim manager is brought in to handle a specific situation – project managing an IT installation, for example – and seeks to transfer his knowledge either to his replacement or other staff managers.

The second is when the interim manager coaches less experienced managers to prepare them to take the next career step. Where a deputy requires a little more time to develop before stepping into a departing manager's shoes, for example, an interim can come in to fill the position for 6 months, with the specific brief to prepare the younger manager to take over. Such interventions can be especially valuable because they provide support to high potential managers without posing a threat to the succession plan.

CASE STUDY

Birky Plastics

Birky Plastics, a subsidiary of the Japanese group Marubeni, brought in an interim manager, while a less experienced internal candidate was being groomed for the job.

'We found we could involve the new man in numerous areas of business without threatening anyone, as they knew he was only there for a short time', Tony Wright, the company's chief executive, told the *Financial Times*.[7]

THE CHIEF EXECUTIVE'S CHOICE

One of the most interesting findings from a 1997 MORI survey commissioned by Boyden Interim Executive Services was that in the majority of cases (78 per cent), the decision to engage an interim manager is made at the very top of the organization by the chief executive. (Second most likely to make the decision are human resources directors.)

Chief executives who have used interim managers also testify to their effectiveness.[8] A key issue, they say, is knowing when to use an interim and when to rely on conventional consultancy.

'We have just put an interim manager into one of our acquired businesses, which means we'll have a "heavyweight, hands-on" manager on site', commented Ian McKinnon, chief executive of British Aluminium. 'This is one of the advantages of interims. You get the benefit of an outsider with a lot of experience handling change at a cost which is roughly half that of management consultancy.'

According to Keith Gilchrist , CEO of the paper and packaging manufacturing company, Field Group plc: 'When you take on interim executives, they're likely to be experienced older hands with an immediate grasp of the job. Younger management consultants are more likely to make most employees feel threatened and this lessens their contribution.'

Dr Colin Gaskill, chief executive of the '600 Group plc (after a 16-year stint at GEC), makes a similar point: 'You use consultants for their specialist know-how. Using them in general management can be a big mistake for many companies. They can turn your business upside down. With the right interim manager you are buying experience. They get the ship afloat fast.

'In his time with us', adds David Sims, former CEO of Nurdin & Peacock plc, 'the interim executive carried out a disposal, took out costs and re-organized the management structure. He certainly didn't just keep the seat warm; he saved us lots of money.'

> *An interim has to call the shots and take responsibility.*

One other point is worth making here. Unlike the consultant, interim managers stand or fall by their track records. Reputation is everything.

As John Pollard, an interim manager for the past 6 years notes, 'An interim has to call the shots and take responsibility. He or she has to be big enough to tell the company if something will not fly and, if it will not listen, must be prepared to walk away. You cannot afford failure as you are only as good as your last job.'[9]

NOTES TO CHAPTER 2

1 Kennedy, Simon, 'Demand for interims steps up', *Headhunters and Human Resources,* 6–12 April 1998.
2 *The ATIES Official Guide to Interim Management*, 1995.
3 Tulgan, Bruce, *Work This Way*, Capstone, 1998.
4 Lacity, M. and Wilcocks, L., 'Best Practice in Information Technology Sourcing', Oxford Executive Research Briefings, Templeton College, Oxford University, 1996.
5 Thorpe, David L., 'Enlisting on-call experts in buyout process', *The Dealmaker's Journal,* Nov/Dec 1997, Vol 32/ No. 3.
6 Brodie, Ian, 'Benefits abound when the boss is just the hired help', *The Times,* 26 September 1996.
7 Kellaway, Lucy, 'Troubleshooters for hire', *Financial Times,* 9 August 1993.
8 MORI Survey, on behalf of Boyden Interim Executive Services, a division of Boyden International, September 1997.
9 Eadie, Alison, 'Stop-gap executives are all the go', *Daily Telegraph*, 12 March 1998.

3

Why companies use interim managers

Flexible resourcing

The business case for interim management

Competitive acceleration

Value for money

Interim vs permanent manager

Interim manager vs consultant

Interims vs outsourcing

Interim manager vs company doctor

One of the advantages of interims is that you get the benefit of an outsider with a lot of experience handling change, at a cost which is roughly half that of management consultancy.[1]

IAN MCKINNON,
Chief Executive of British Aluminium

In the past, difficult, short-term corporate assignments were filled in a 'hit or miss' fashion. In many cases, already over-stretched senior executives or inexperienced middle managers would be asked to take on additional responsibilities. Or the project, regardless of its strategic importance to the business, would have to wait until the appropriate person was free to carry it forward. Alternatively, the company would wait for the right external candidate to pop up on the 'old boys network.'

With the high costs of permanent employment at or near to board level, an expensive commodity, the operating environment has a much sharper focus today. Meeting the costs of pensions, company cars, incentives and golden handshakes, makes bringing in additional management resource costly, particularly when the need is just for a short-term project.

> *The interim moves on without any additional cost to the host company.*

In America and some parts of Europe, the trend towards interim managers represents an increasing recognition among blue-chip companies that interims can be used to provide additional (and often highly specialized) executive capacity on a temporary basis. These individuals are brought in to meet a clearly defined objective.

A key benefit is that, unlike a permanent member of staff, once the objective has been met, the interim moves on without any additional cost to the host company.

In other parts of Europe and Asia, however, the use of interim managers has been slower to take off. In some areas, the market may now be ready for the technique, whilst in others it may already be happening under the guise of consultancy or some other name.

FLEXIBLE RESOURCING

An important point to realize about interim management is that it is simply one option for handling staffing needs. In other words, it is one tool – or solution – among several at the organization's disposal. Because it is still a relatively new resourcing tool, however, it is not always given the consideration it merits.

Surveys, for example, show that those companies that have not used interim managers before are more likely to turn to familiar – albeit often less effective – solutions.

These may include:

- external appointment
- internal secondment
- management consultancy
- outsourcing
- company doctor.

One of these deserves special attention here. Some people, and even some specialist interim firms, seem to regard interim management as nothing more than an offshoot of the market for independent management consultants. These people do not draw too much of a distinction between the two, often lumping them together as though they were two parts of the same market. (This confusion may go some way to explaining why estimates of the size of the interim market vary so widely.)

But, to regard interim managers as just a special, hands-on variety of consultants, in our opinion, underestimates their potential contribution. It also ignores the fact that the two roles require a different set of behaviours and skills.

As John Hird, managing director of the UK interim firm, Albermarle explains: 'They are very different disciplines. Unlike consultants, who typically make recommendations and offer advice and guidance on how to achieve a particular objective, interim managers are able to walk into a company and take charge of a situation immediately.'

Some interims do take on consultancy work in addition to interim assignments, but most are very clear about the difference between the two. At present the role of the interim can, and often does, overlap with that of the consultant, but in part this is because in the past, organizations have used consultants for a wide variety of tasks for which it would be more appropriate – and less costly – to use interims.

As Martin Wood, head of Boyden Interim Executive, points out: 'Before interims can prove themselves, chief executives must be brave enough to use them in the first place. It is a much easier choice to call in a big brand name consultant. Many companies are using interims for the first time. If they have a bad experience they won't use them again.'[2]

As Alison Eadie noted in the *Daily Telegraph*:[3] 'The problem is that not many people know what interim managers do. They are high-class temps with a wealth of business experience, of mature years (as opposed to wet-behind-the-ears consultants), carrying no overheads as they work for themselves and prepared to roll up their sleeves and do a job rather than just advise.

'They come into a company for an average of six months to fill a temporary vacancy or carry out a specific project, help with a sudden overload of work or do a spot of trouble-shooting. They are generally overqualified for their interim jobs, having reached more senior levels when on the corporate pay-roll.'

Despite their fundamental differences, there are instances where the use of an interim manager complements the work of consultants. 'Interims are quite frequently following consultants into organizations to implement their recommendations', says John Hird.

The pros and cons of using an interim manager in place of a management consultant are discussed later. Suffice it to say here that they are two different resourcing options. Whether, in time, the two roles move closer to one another will probably depend on the impact that interim management makes on the traditional market for consultancy.

In reality, however, the interim role is probably closer to that of a company doctor than it is to that of a consultant.

Raising awareness

A 1997 MORI Survey commissioned by Boyden Interim Executive, indicates that the full potential of interim management is still not widely understood. While 75 per cent of the participating organizations were familiar with the term 'interim executive', the other 25 per cent had no knowledge of it. Moreover, nearly 50 per cent of those familiar with the term categorized it as temporary/short-term contract work.

More encouragingly, over 40 per cent of respondents understood it to mean 'the provision of senior executives at or near board level as an alternative to management consultants, or to implement change for a certain period of change'.

A separate survey carried out on behalf of the UK human resources consultancy Greythorn found that 37 per cent of companies currently used interim managers, while 63 per cent did not.[4] Many of those that do not currently use interims admitted that long-term management absences led to overworked key staff and disrupted productivity. This, the report's authors suggested, was an encouraging sign for the future of interim management. At least companies are aware that traditional approaches to staffing are no longer enough.

Britannia Life

In the early 1990s, Britannia Life hired an interim manager to help it absorb the acquisition of another financial services company. 'We needed a thorough review, and needed it quickly', Peter Burdon, the company's managing director, explained to the *Financial Times*.[5]

Burdon opted for an interim rather than a consultant because the latter are 'isolated and sell solutions. They also run up all sorts of additional costs. An interim manager is a fixed cost.'

The company was offered a choice between two candidates for the assignment. The successful applicant started work within a week and subsequently joined Britannia's permanent staff.

THE BUSINESS CASE FOR INTERIM MANAGEMENT

To understand why companies are now starting to use interim managers more frequently, it is important to consider the options from their perspective. What is surprising, given the challenges faced by businesses in the past two decades, is that the potential benefits of the interim concept are only now starting to be widely recognized.

The business case for using interims is persuasive. However, it has not been terribly well made in the past. Interim management seems to have been the victim of poor communication.

'In The Netherlands and Scandinavia, interim management is well-established and distinct from consultancy', noted Alison Eadie[6] in the *Daily Telegraph*. But in other countries, especially the UK: 'If it is to be elevated to a separate discipline and a separate source of income for recruitment firms, it is going to have to explain itself better.'

The point is well made, although interim management is now beginning to come into its own in certain national markets. In Britain, where it has been slower to take off than in some other European countries, word of mouth remains a potent marketing tool.

The firms which specialize in placing interims have to take some of the blame here – as do management journalists, who have a tendency to be cynical. Despite the fact that the idea has been around now for more than 20 years, most of the articles written on the subject, and even the marketing materials of firms that specialize in placing interims, simply re-hash the same old arguments for and against.

> *Interim management seems to have been the victim of poor communication.*

On the positive side, interims can step into a post at short notice and 'hit the deck running'. On the negative side, they are seen as expensive by comparison with permanent staff (though typically cheaper than consultants) – costing upwards of £400 a day. Whether you think the positive outweighs the negative will depend on your point of view and particular set of circumstances. But, what undoubtedly worked against the wider use of interims is a lingering suspicion that someone who comes in as an interim manager may be seeking to turn a temporary role into a full-time job. This is largely irrelevant to the real issue.

The question that companies should be asking themselves today is whether they are prepared to take a broad view of the role of interim managers, or whether they see them simply as a stop-gap solution to a crisis. Put another way, the challenge facing companies now is recognizing the strategic resource that interim management offers rather than viewing it narrowly as a tactical option.

Naturally, there will be situations where an interim manager is the sensible solution to fill an empty post that has arisen because of an emergency, or some other unforeseen circumstance. The idea of a 'safe pair of hands' to come in at short notice will always be appealing in such a situation. However, that is not the most effective way to use an interim manager.

As the notion of 'organizational agility' becomes more widely understood in the next few years, the potential benefits of interim management will also be more widely recognized.

John Murray, head of PA Consulting's Global Interim Management practice, agrees. 'Interim managers have traditionally been seen either as the people who hold the fort or as the last throw of the dice before the liquidators arrive. This is no longer the case. Agile companies have come to realize that interims can bring instant extra horsepower, enabling them to surge past their plodding competitors.'

With its consultancy pedigree, PA applies the logic of consultants. An interim manager can provide:

● competitive acceleration
● value for money.

COMPETITIVE ACCELERATION

The first point, says Murray, is that 'if you try to resource all of your growth and innovation from inside, you will fail because no single company has a monopoly of wisdom or insight – or indeed resource. There is a concept called acceleration which will, for the sake of a relatively short-term, albeit slightly expensive, investment, take you past your competitor within your particular market if you choose the right moment.'

> *Agile companies have come to realize that interims can bring instant extra horsepower.*

That acceleration can be in many forms, he says. For example, it can come from:

● technological development

- re-organizing a company's supply chain
- aligning its systems exactly with your business process instead of inexactly
- through developing a new commercial proposition. For example, direct banking and direct insurance wiped out intermediaries overnight.

'We think interims can deliver that. Not always and probably not at the bottom half of the market – but certainly the top level of our business which is the top 50 per cent.'

This can be especially effective when a company is experiencing poor performance. One American interim firm uses a baseball analogy. It goes like this:

'*Scenario:* An organization has stumbled; losing market share, lost a critical major account, or otherwise stubbed its toe. It could be and should be, doing better. *Solution:* The single best cure for existing managerial non-performance is to insert a hard-throwing relief pitcher – the interim manager.'

In future, this offers significant competitive advantage. The capability to help organizations accelerate past their competitors brings interim management into direct competition with management consulting. John Murray has no qualms about this.

'As I've said to our management consultants, if you think you are in the same business as an interim, come and try it. But, you will find you get into awfully difficult situations for a consultant; situations where you have to make decisions that commit millions of pounds. You, rather than the client, have to choose one technology over another technology. With an interim assignment, you're the man and the shareholders will fire you if they don't like the results. It isn't like that in consulting.

'As an interim manager, your job starts with a recommendation from the consultant and then you get on and do it. You are drawing on lots of management expertise which you've gathered in your career, drawing on not so much intellectual analysis but intuitive sense of this will work in this company or it won't work given the climate or the culture.

'We see interim management as a consequence of consulting. Consultants may point out the route but interims "walk the walk".'

VALUE FOR MONEY

The second compelling value proposition for interim management, according to the PA Consulting Group, is value for money. This may, at first sight, seem an odd argument. The typical reaction of a divisional general manager faced with the idea of paying £1000 a day for an outsider, for example, is not immediately to think in terms of value for money, particularly if he is paying the person who had the job previously no more than £50 000 or £60 000 a year.

But, there are many hidden costs associated with a permanent appointment which do not apply to an interim manager see Table 3.1.

Senior managers in large organizations are not always productively employed. There is a propensity, especially during relatively stable times, for their time to be occupied by what can be described as 'corporate activity', such as writing positioning papers, going to conferences and attending industry committee meetings.

Table 3.1 Hidden costs associated with a permanent executive

Permanent executive	Interim manager
Pension contribution	N/a
Company car	N/a
Secretary or PA	N/a
Paid holiday	N/a
Sickness pay	N/a
Training courses	N/a
Bonuses	N/a
Stock options	N/a
Severance package	N/a

INTERIM vs PERMANENT MANAGER

The most obvious alternative to using an interim manager is to opt for the traditional resourcing route of either hiring an additional manager or borrowing – seconding – one from elsewhere in the organization. Both of these alternatives involve a permanent member of staff.

In the past, when companies had some spare managerial capacity, it was common to draft in someone from another part of the organization to cover for unexpected departures, maternity leave and the like. If necessary, this also provided a breathing space while the company recruited a permanent replacement.

However, today's lean organizations do not have this luxury. Increasingly, the pressure is on them to eliminate idle hands among the management population. This process has been underway now for some time. Companies have tended to attack the fat by reducing headcount. This is placing pressure on managers to manage their own time more effectively.

The logical next phase is to try to streamline what managers actually do to make them more effective resources. This is likely to see an attack on unproductive corporate activity such as unnecessary meetings, pointless reports, and other bureaucratic wastage.[7]

As PA's John Murray explains: 'We are trying to educate chief executives into realizing that management labour costs are semi fixed rather than fixed; to get into the habit of carrying less management than they need – perhaps having a management team on a virtual basis. I noticed in Brussels, for example, that a

> *There is no energy dissipated on career manoeuvring.*

number of companies share an accountant. They are relatively small companies, they can't afford an FD [finance director] on their own, so four companies share one. Used strategically, interim management can achieve the same effect.'

Permanent senior managers can be significantly less productive than their interim counterparts. Interim managers have no time to join in the less productive behaviours that are endemic to corporate life. As a result, there is no energy dissipated on career manoeuvring, defending lost causes or demonstrating their indispensability. Their diaries tend not to be filled with conferences, seminars or industry meetings. They do not take paid time off for holidays. Nor do they spend 15 days a year acting as a non-executive director on other companies' boards. Best of all, when the job in hand is done, they leave quietly. There is no compensation or on-going pension contributions. They are productive assets all of the time.

Key advantages of the interim manager:

1 Senior management defines in clear terms what the goals of the assignment are.
2 The interim is selected for the assignment on the basis of his ability – expertise and experience – to deliver those specific goals.

3 The interim manager's only agenda is to pursue, direct , measure, report, coach toward, and accomplish those goals.

4 Interim managers have little interest in a company's internal politics. They act as a reminder to senior and middle management that sales and profits (not personal agendas) are the driving goals of the company.

5 The interim manager's fee doesn't upset the internal salary structure of existing managers, so there's no whining or finger-pointing as things return to normal once the interim departs.

Interim managers represent a 'lean' resource. Because they are paid by the day, they have to add value daily which gives a sharp edge to everything they do. They are hired for a specific project and have to work full steam ahead until that task is completed. There is no wastage.

Says John Murray of PA Consulting: 'Many companies staff up for things that may happen. They prefer to have extra people on the pay-roll than to have to go looking for them. On the other hand if you are carrying the fat, that's very expensive. So our argument is, keep it slim and then out reach for your interim to address the peaks of work flow which you cannot possibly match with permanent resources.'

'When their job is completed the interim leaves, without compensation or on-going pension costs. Interims are productive assets not expensive liabilities.'

INTERIM MANAGER vs CONSULTANT

Although interim management is now gaining much wider acceptance and understanding in its own right, there is still confusion in some quarters about how it differs from consultancy. In a sense, to explain what interim management is, it is also necessary to clarify what it is not. It is not a form of consultancy (although it can be used to complement the work of consultants).

The key distinction that is usually made between the role of the consultant and the role of the interim manager is that the former makes recommendations but does not get involved with implementation, while the latter does. The consultant has an advisory relationship with clients' staff; interim managers take line management responsibility, frequently for an entire operating unit or department, and sometimes for the whole company. To put it another way, interim managers are doers, while consultants are advisers.

A MORI survey commissioned by Boyden Interim Executive,[8] asked companies about their experiences of consultancy and interim management. It found that the key advantages of interim managers were seen to be:

- greater depth of management experience
- better implementation
- faster achievement of the required results
- and greater commitment than was generally the case with consultants.

Keith Gilchrist, CEO of Field Group, a leading paper and packaging manufacturer, has a clear approach to deciding when to hire a management consultant rather than an interim executive.

'When we need specialist advice, for example to analyse areas of malfunction or to write a new computer program, we use management consultants. When we want to implement change, such as standardizing order processing throughout our ten factories, we use interim management.'[9]

Gilchrist observes: 'When you take on an interim manager he's likely to be an experienced older hand with an immediate grasp of the job. Younger management consultants are more likely to make most employees feel threatened and this lessens their contribution.'

But, there are also other fundamental differences between the two roles. Consultants are ultimately responsible and account-able to the consultancy firm to which they belong. The interim manager, on the other hand becomes a part – albeit only for the duration of the assignment – of the management team. As such, he or she reports directly to the senior managers, and often the chief executive in person.

> When you hire a younger manager, you are investing in their potential, but when a client hires an interim manager, they are paying for their track record.

According to Richard Foot, of PA Con-sulting Group's Interim Management Division, the difference between an interim manager and a traditional management consultant is ownership.

'Interim managers report to a client directly and are normally the immediate authority for client employees,' he says. 'They will get their hands dirty and defend their own decisions for the time that they are there. They are one of the team and stand or fall accordingly.'

Another key difference between many consultants and interim managers is experience. Even though the consulting partner who initially visits the company is a highly experienced – and often highly polished – manager in his own right, in many cases most of the work is carried out by business school graduates in their twenties. Whether this is a good or bad thing depends on your point of view. The well-heeled young men and women who gather information, carry out all sorts of analysis and evaluations are generally bright in the academic sense of the word. Inevitably, however, they are less well schooled in the university of life.

Interim managers, on the other hand, are typically in their 40s or 50s. Any younger, it is argued, and they are don't have the experience or gravitas to perform the role effectively. Many companies that use interims actually admit that they find the presence of a few grey hairs reassuring.

Richard Foot confirms the point: 'Experience is very important for an interim. When you hire a younger manager, you are investing in their potential, but when a client hires an interim manager, they are paying for their track record. That's an important difference.'

Consultants typically derive their authority from the internal client, usually a senior manager, but an interim must be able to walk into an office on day one and take charge. Part of the interim's success, then, depends on the ability to plug directly into the culture and open doors for himself.

Research carried out at Exeter University indicates that interim managers are more efficient and cost-effective than consultants in many situations. The survey, which was commissioned by the recruitment firm Barton International, found that some 83 per cent of respondents said value for money was a distinct advantage of interim managers, with just 40 per cent saying the same of consultants.

> *An interim must be able to walk into an office on day one and take charge.*

So, why don't more companies use interims rather than consultants?

That's a very good question, and one that a growing number of companies are starting to ask themselves.

INTERIMS vs OUTSOURCING

The idea behind outsourcing is as old as business itself. Basically, it is a response to the question 'Which areas of activity are central to our business, and which can be best be performed by external suppliers?' It arises from the recognition that no company can excel at everything. Areas involving competencies that are not central to what the business does are best left to those who specialize in them.

What has changed in recent years, however, is the understanding of which functions can be sensibly removed from the core business and sourced from outside. In the past, for example, many administrative activities were seen as part and parcel of running the business. As a result, it simply didn't occur to companies to outsource areas such as pay-roll, delivery of finished goods, and secretarial services. That has now changed as it has become fashionable for companies to focus on their core activities – those which provide competitive advantage.

In the case of key strategic projects such as the implementation of major IT systems, companies often outsource their needs at present simply because they lack the in-house capability to manage the installation. The use of a highly experienced interim IT director, however, can provide an alternative to outsourcing a company's IT capability.

In many cases, the use of an interim manager to assess the options, negotiate with contractors and manage the handover can be highly beneficial. Research has shown that many outsourcing contracts in recent years were entered into without a proper consideration of the issues. Poorly negotiated outsourcing contracts can cost the client company literally millions of pounds in additional expense.

Mary Lacity and Leslie Willcocks, two academics at Oxford University, researched IT sourcing decisions in 40 US and UK companies.

Of a total of 61 IT outsourcing decisions, they found that 34 (56 per cent) were successful, 14 (23 per cent) were unsuccessful, and in 13 cases (21 per cent) it was too early to tell. (For the purposes of evaluating the impact of these decisions, the key

success indicator was defined in terms of 'achieving antici-
pated cost savings'.)

Lacity and Willcocks identify a number of lessons for managing the outsourcing process:

- Right sourcing is selective sourcing. Success therefore
  depends on a great deal of management attention.
- Tailored contracts are better than 'strategic' partnerships. Too
  often the rhetoric of strategic partnership fails to translate into
  contractual terms, which should reflect shared risk and
  rewards. As a result, many such agreements favour the vendor.
- Short-term contracts are better than long-term contracts.
- Outsourcing often involves substantial hidden costs. Unan-
  ticipated costs were a recurring feature of many of the deals
  studied. These often result from weaknesses in evaluation
  prior to signing contracts.
- Internal IT departments should be encouraged to bid against
  external suppliers. Senior managers often exclude internal IT
  departments from the bidding process. Many believe that: 'If
  my IT managers could do it, they would have done it
  already.'

A number of comments from the report are also highly instructive. In particular, Lacity and Willcocks observe: 'All sourcing
decisions should begin with the perception of IT as a business
enabler ... the power of information technology lies fundamentally in its integration with business operations.'

Perhaps most illuminating of all, however, are comments
from those involved in the decision making process. The logic
of bringing in an interim who has successfully negotiated outsourcing contracts is simply common sense.

As one IT director observed: 'A user will sign one or two of
these contracts during his/her career: vendors sign one or two
a week.' An experienced interim can help redress the balance.

Carters Gold Medal Soft Drinks

One company that has benefited from the use of an interim manager is Carters Gold Medal Soft Drinks, part of the Swiss food group, Hero. What started as a short appraisal of delivery methods and possible outsourcing options led to the complete replacement of the distribution arm of the company – saving Carter's around £1 million per annum from a total distribution spend of around £7 million.

Carters distributes its products direct to supermarkets and, via wholesalers, to a number of small retail outlets. The company brought in interim manager, Jon Tipping, through the interim specialist Albermarle. Initially, brought in on a 4-week contract, Tipping was eventually retained for 4 months.

As Carters managing director explains: 'For various reasons connected with our history we were using a dedicated fleet of owner drivers supplemented by spot hire, which incurred a lot of wasted vehicle space and mileage. Jon Tipping's brief was to evaluate the various quotations we had obtained from national logistics companies to replace our fleet. In the event he helped us forward to a better solution.'

As well as evaluating the quotations – which confirmed that the company's in-house distribution operation was too costly – Tipping researched the problems facing the company in different regions around the country. As a result, Carters eventually signed a series of regionally based contracts with dedicated transport operators.

INTERIM MANAGER vs COMPANY DOCTOR

The role of the interim manager is most akin to that of the company doctor. According to the UK interim firm Executives on Assignments (EoA): 'Interim managers have advanced from acting as mere stop-gaps. They are increasingly called in as company doctors to improve performance or put right corporate deficiencies. As in the US (where they are an established way of corporate life) their greater potential is now recognized and they are hired for tasks such as turning round loss-making subsidiaries, reorganizing entire departments, or reducing corporate debt.'

But, whereas in many cases a company doctor will bring in a team to handle a recovery situation, the interim typically operates on his own, and with limited powers.

For this reason, the ability of interim managers to tackle full-scale corporate recoveries is limited. What will be interesting to watch in the next few years is

> *They are increasingly called in as company doctors to improve performance.*

whether the larger interim specialists are able to start putting together carefully chosen teams of interims who might be brought in to handle a corporate recovery – perhaps replacing the top management team and acting under the auspices of non-executive directors.

Company doctors, however, are in short supply. PA's Stuart Cain worked with a leading company doctor before joining PA's interim operation. He says: 'Company doctor is just an extreme and rather specific version of an interim manager in a loss-making situation. Company doctor sounds a bit more glamorous doesn't it? It's also the top man. There are relatively few recognized company doctors in the UK. There are, let us say, a couple of thousand interim managers. Company doctors, you are probably talking about a couple of hundred.'

Interestingly, one American interim firm describes the interim role as that of 'management fence builder' – since it's always better to have a fence at the edge of a cliff than an ambulance waiting at the bottom'.

NOTES TO CHAPTER 3

1 MORI survey on behalf of Boyden Interim Executive Services, September, 1997.

2 Eadie, Alison, 'Stop-gap executives are all the go', *Daily Telegraph*, 12 March 1998.

3 Eadie, Alison, 'Interim solution cuts company costs', *Daily Telegraph*, 22 January 1998.

4 The Greythorn Report, 'Interim Management Myths Exploded', November 1997.

5 Kellaway, Lucy, 'Troubleshooters for hire', *Financial Times*, 9 August 1993.

6 Eadie, Alison, 'Interim solution cuts company costs', *Daily Telegraph*, 22 January 1998.

7 Several books have appeared recently on this very subject, including Michael Champy's sequel to *Re-engineering the Corporation* called *Re-engineering Management*. In it, Champy argues, that the BPR revolution was all about re-engineering processes within organizations. But, to date, it has left management processes largely untouched.

8 MORI Survey, on behalf of Boyden Interim Executive Services, a division of Boyden International, 1997.

9 Altman, Wilf, 'Executive temps on the rise', *The Times*, 5 December 1996.

Why do people become interim managers?

Flexing not temping

The portfolio people

The new professionals

Ten myths about interim managers

The interim manager may be a victim and beneficiary of the blitzkrieg of 'downsizing'. He is also the 'portfolio executive' identified by Charles Handy the management commentator.[1]

MARGARET COLES, *Sunday Times*

One of the first questions many people ask about interims is who are they? This is often closely followed by: Where did they come from? There is a lingering feeling that perhaps they are 'displaced' managers who are unable to get 'real jobs'.

Charles Russam, head of the UK interim firm Russam GMS, admits that the role has not always enjoyed the status that it deserves. 'For a long time there was a feeling with interim managers – as with consultants – that perhaps people were doing this because they couldn't get a proper job', he says. 'But, that's fading as people realize there's a pool of highly qualified managers who are available for hire on a short-term basis.'

What research has been done suggests that interims come from a wide variety of industries and circumstances. What all have in common is a background in professional management and many years experience.

What we do know about them is that they tend to be mature individuals. Some 60 per cent of interims in a 1997 survey by the UK interim firm, Russam GMS, were aged between 45 and 55, while 38 per cent were between 48 and 53. Most are men; women currently make up less than 5 per cent.[2]

The same survey found that two-fifths took up interim management after being made redundant, but nearly a third reported that they did not want to go back to a permanent job.

There is a paradox here. As Margaret Coles observed in the *Sunday Times* recently: 'The interim manager may be a victim and beneficiary of the blitzkrieg of "downsizing". He is also the "portfolio executive" identified by Charles Handy the management commentator.'[3]

What is clear is that the status of interim managers as a professional group is beginning to be more widely understood. In Britain, for example, for a while in the mid-1990s they were often confused either with 'displaced executives' who were filling in while they looked for a permanent position, or the much talked about 'deadwood' that was being stripped out of British business. Many of the companies that have used interims now recognize that they are neither.

In reality, interim managers will always be overqualified for the assignments they take on. The interim role is 'overkill by overskill', one experienced interim says. Where they have come from is much less important than what they can do.

FLEXING NOT TEMPING

Today, there is a new breed of highly experienced, hands-on managers available to come into organizations at short notice, and for a limited time, to implement change and manage challenging projects. Interim managers, however, should not to be confused with 'temps' in the traditional sense of the word. There is little doubt that the use of flexible staffing options – through part-time working and contracting is on the increase. From the employers' perspective, it provides less rigid staffing, and often cost savings since traditional benefits such as holiday and sick pay are avoided. Not everyone sees this as a positive development.

> Interim managers will always be overqualified for the assignments they take on.

Research carried out by the outplacement specialists, Sanders & Sidney, however, suggests that many of those in more junior roles resent the imposition of fixed contracts by employers as it makes it difficult to plan pensions, mortgages and holidays. Some 76 per cent of job-seekers in the survey also complained that it had an adverse effect on the company culture, making team-building more difficult and creating uncertainty.

Indeed, there is plenty of evidence to suggest that unscrupulous employers have used this trend to exploit vulnerable sections of the working population. At the same time, in certain sectors, such as IT, where there are skills shortages, the move to contracting in particular has created a highly lucrative source of employment. But, interim managers are an altogether different phenomenon.

Recruitment companies which specialize in interim assignments say that for a select band of very senior individuals, short-term contracts are an appealing option. These individuals – typically in their late 40s or early 50s – find the new way of working can provide a lifestyle that is the envy of their full-time counterparts, with periods of intense work followed by time to reflect and pursue other interests.

PA Consulting Group was one of a number of companies which pioneered interim management in the UK in the early 1990s, as a response to what it saw as a growing demand in both the private and public sectors for the services of high-quality executives to fill board level and senior management positions for temporary periods.

Typical projects, it says, include managing acquisitions, merger and demerger situations, company turnarounds and helping organizations through important transitions. Unlike consultants, who usually advise on what needs to be done, the interim manager is involved with implementation, taking on the responsibilities of a line manager to get the job done.

While some managers will switch in and out of the interim role as their careers progress, it is only exceptionally competent managers who can perform the role effectively. The reason why this is not yet as widely understood as it should be is to do with other developments in the labour market over the past two decades.

A number of factors have masked the true nature of the

> *It is only exceptionally competent managers who can perform the role effectively.*

interim market. Two recessions, in the early 1980s and then in the early 1990s, gave added impetus to a process that was already under way – the emergence of the freelance business professional.

THE PORTFOLIO PEOPLE

To understand where the interim manager fits into the new world of work, it is necessary to survey the changing career landscape. The biggest change to take place to management jobs in recent years is the transition from corporate employment to self-employment – from 'sheltered jobs' to 'contingent work'.

The most obvious indication of the rise of the freelance business professional is the growing number of independent consultants. Not so long ago, it would have seemed odd for an individual to carry out consultancy for his or her former employer and other companies. But, today such arrangements are commonplace. What successive recessions and the downsizing that has taken place in recent years have done is to push a lot of redundant executives onto the job market.

What has occurred is a massive exodus of white-collar workers from what were once regarded as secure 'jobs for life' into the altogether more precarious world of self-employment. The fact is that some of those who have been displaced are very much more suited to their new roles than others.

In truth, though, downsizing simply speeded up the movement from the single company career to the portfolio career. What redundancy has done for many of the more capable managers is to liberate them from their corporate cells.

Today, there are many more people operating as self-employed satellites orbiting around larger organizations. These are Charles Handy's portfolio people. Often lumped together, these people perform a wide range of different professional roles.

At present, the independent consultancy sector is populated with all sorts of people who didn't expect to be there. Many decided to become consultants not because they wanted to but because they couldn't find another job. In other cases, their former employer offered them some consultancy work to get them started. Some of them, to their great surprise, have discovered that they are actually very good at it and thoroughly enjoy their new employment status. Others are less comfortable – and less well suited to the role. Only a small percentage of them have the necessary skills, experience and attitude to become true interim managers.

> *Downsizing speeded up the movement from single company career to portfolio career.*

Buoyant market for independents

A recent survey of 5000 executives carried out by IMCOR,[4] the US interim company, found that managers are encountering a buoyant market for temporary assignments.

The survey also showed that 30 per cent of assignments convert to 'permanent' positions, often offering a flexible bridge back to permanent employment for those who want it.

For some, interim assignments and consultancy provide a valuable stop-gap while they are between full-time positions, offering the opportunity to extend skills and experience and earn an income while making the transition.

But the survey also suggested that as many as a third of the respondents were already working as professional interims. For them, the dawning of the new employment era has brought enormous benefits. These are people who have taken to the new role like ducks to water and have no desire to go back to permanent jobs.

CASE STUDY

ServiceTeam

When the sale of a major part of the business at Cardinal Group plc ended, so did Peter Dunckley's job as a director. 'I knew it was coming', he says, 'but it still came as a bit of a shock to find myself with time on my hands. At the time I was looking for a new and fresh challenge. A friend of mine said that he had completed a number of assignments as an interim manager and suggested I try it. I approached a few interim firms and after a few months got my first assignment through PA Consulting.'

A chartered accountant, Peter is in his early 50s and worked on his first assignment as an interim manager with ServiceTeam Ltd, which has recently taken over the provision of local services – including refuse collection, transport, street cleaning, school meals and building repairs – from Lambeth Council.

'I was brought in to set up the new accounting system and financial controls', he says. 'All the accounting for the services was previously looked after by Lambeth Central Finance. We are responsible for paying the 2000 employees that ServiceTeam has taken over, plus all the other accounting matters. I came in with a blank sheet of paper into an empty office with three operations managers to set up various services and put the finance function in place.'

Peter says he enjoyed the challenge, and would certainly like to do more interim assignments. 'I have only two concerns about working as an interim manager', he says. 'When you take on a role you get totally embroiled in it as if you were a full-time member of staff. You have a desire to see your labours in the early months come to fruition, but, of course, you may not get the chance because the changes you put in place might take a while to bear fruit and by then you may have moved on to the next assignment.'

His other concern? 'I haven't worked in a position in a subsidiary company for a long time and find it quite frustrating having someone at a parent company level to report to rather than just doing it my way.'

The insecurity of the job doesn't bother him, he says, although he would consider staying with an assignment company on a permanent basis if the terms were right.

THE NEW PROFESSIONALS

Interim management is a new profession, but one that is rapidly gaining ground. It is an indication of its growing status that today it is even taught at business school.

Offered in co-operation with the Raad voor Interim Management firm (RIM), the Erasmus Graduate School of Business, in Rotterdam offers a 'Master Class in Interim Management'. It consists of a series of four 2-day modules and covers a range of issues including: the role of the interim manager in change process; changing organizational cultures; reflective professionalism; and conflict management.

Still small in number at present, as companies become more aware of this strategic resourcing option over the next few years, interim management is likely to have an increasing impact on the way that companies operate. Today, they probably number a few thousand managers in countries around the world. But their numbers are growing as other like-minded people recognize that there is a different career path open to them.

For these people, a series of events – some inside and others outside of their control – have clicked like cosmic tumblers and the door to a new world of work has swung open. For any number of reasons, they were persuaded to try interim management, and having tried it and succeeded, they have decided they like it. Many of them talk about being 'freed' from the constraints of corporate life. Interestingly, too, when they look back on their previous careers, several of those who have been interim managers for some time say that they were never entirely comfortable in a permanent job and now understand why they didn't fit into the corporate mould.

Interim assignments are also often the best insurance against redundancy. Sid Burrows, for example, a logistics and operations expert, was made redundant at 39 and became an interim at 40.

'When I was made redundant, my first reaction was to get another full-time job, which I did', he says. 'But I could see that I was going to be out of a job again in about 18 months. When I looked back over my career, I realized that what I was really good at was managing change, but once the change was in place, a different type of manager was needed. That meant I was going to be looking for a new job every 2 years.'

> *They were never entirely comfortable in a permanent job.*

His response was to offer his services as an interim, even though at the time the concept was still in its infancy in the UK. The first few assignments came from networking, but that changed with the advent of the specialist recruiters. Because they were looking to fill senior management appointments, too, Sid Burrows found his age was an asset.

'I was put forward for an assignment at Mercury Communications where there were other candidates who were younger and had better academic qualifications. But, what the client saw in me was a lot of experience. He knew that he could trust me to do the job.'

A 3-month assignment for Mercury turned into 3 years. Now 50, Burrows is an established interim manager specializing in operations and logistics and has no desire to take on a full-time post.

Some of the people we talked to have been working as

interim managers now for more than a decade and have a track record of successful assignments under their belt that is well into double figures.

They include people like Kim James, who proudly boasts that he has had 54 jobs in the past 10 years – ranging from 15 months to two days. His CV is three pages long and reads like a *Who's Who* of the corporate world, with stints at companies including British Airways, Grand Metropolitan, MFI and Scottish Hydro Electric. Not so long ago, his colourful career history might have been frowned upon, but today it is his calling card.

James estimates his interview to job ratio is around one in five, which means he has probably attended over 250 job interviews in his career. But his job tally really shot up 8 years ago when – at the age of 41 – he began working on interim assignments. Yet, even before that James was a dedicated job-hopper.

'I came from an unconventional background', he says. 'I left school at 15 and went to work in a factory, eventually becoming a shop steward. I went back to education and did a postgraduate degree in Personnel Management – equivalent to an MSc. From there I did various jobs in personnel always with top companies, but after a while I found that I was in the wrong jobs – ones which weren't sufficiently stimulating intellectually.

'That was back in the 1980s when manufacturing was struggling and I could see what was happening. I saw myself then as a capable HR manager but really a manufacturing person. I had to change my profile, change with the times. I went into consultancy and then landed a job as an interim manager. Now, I use every job-seeking tool at my disposal to get assignments.'

When we spoke to him, Mike Measures, another professional interim manager, had spent the previous 6 months working in Barcelona. The assignment – working as a financial controller at the Spanish subsidiary of a UK manufacturing company – came up at short notice.

'They wanted a Spanish-speaking accountant with experience of a UK plc', he explained. 'I was the finance director in my last company, and I've worked all over the world including Barcelona, so the job fitted me like a glove. I was in position in less than 10 days.'

With the contract approaching a successful conclusion, Measures was looking forward to a well-earned break to do some scuba diving. Meanwhile, Tony Cox, another interim, had just completed a 9-month contract with Northern Foods as European sales and marketing director. That leaves him free to spend a month or so indulging his passion for sailing.

With periods away from home and a question mark over the next job, however, the role doesn't suit everyone, especially those with young families and large mortgages.

'It's not everybody's cup of tea', PA's Richard Foot agrees. 'When we interview people, we make sure they are approaching it with the right mental attitude and aren't just doing it because they're desperate for work. We can't guarantee continuity of assignments, and some people don't like the insecurity involved.'

Others seem to thrive on it.

CASE STUDY

Interim solutions for the NHS

Recruiting and committing to an individual in a hurry, can carry considerable risks, which is why an increasing number of organizations are deciding to take their time in appointing new executives and in the meantime employ the services of an interim manager.

The West Berkshire Priority Care Service NHS Trust was established in 1994 and is responsible for providing a complex range of health services over a wide geographical area. These services include community hospitals and mental health services and hospital-based mental health services, specialist learning disability services, together with a range of health screening and education programmes. Employing 2300 staff. The Trust has an annual income of around £56 million.

The Finance Director had been in his position since the Trust was formed. A well-respected executive, colleagues were sad to see him leave to take up a more senior role within the National Health Service – a position that required he work only his minimum notice period.

Finding a suitable replacement wasn't going to happen overnight and the Trust's chief executive, Gareth Cruddace, wanted to take time to appoint the right individual for this key role within the organization.

PA Consulting Group's Interim Management Practice was given the recruitment brief, and the company's interim management division asked to find someone to step in between departure and appointment of FD.

Philip Sheward was selected for the assignment. Philip has over 25 years' financial management experience in large organizations – the last 10 years at board level. More recently, he has been operating as an interim manager, working in both the public and private sectors and of particular benefit to his new clients was his recent assignment for another NHS trust.

The West Berkshire Priority Care Service NHS Trust was no stranger to the concept of hiring interim managers. Chief Executive Gareth Cruddace had called on this resource on two previous occasions, the first when setting up the Trust, to determine whether it was best to hire a personnel director with specific experience of the NHS or draw on the wider experience of an individual from the private sector. The interim personnel director who was on board for over 12 months was not an NHS person and convinced him that an 'outsider' would have more to offer.

A second interim manager was hired in an effort to avoid any potential empire building by a permanent employee. The role was director of information – a department which had yet to be set up. 'We thought it would be useful to have a manager who would not be bound by thinking of the kind of department he would like to run in the long term. The issues in setting up the department included whether to outsource various activities, and we did not want strategy to be decided by someone tainted by self-interest.'

The Trust's most recent interim manager, Philip Sheward, spent 5 months in the organization acting as FD, and has now handed over to his permanent replacement.

> *We did not want strategy to be decided by someone tainted by self-interest.*

Speaking of his time at the Trust, Sheward comments: 'Given that the Trust's finances are sound, I was able to spend time focusing on the steady improvement to procedures and processes.

'Although the Trust had successfully tackled a number of issues during its first 3 years, the time was right for an 'outsider' to bring a fresh perspective. Senior managers were receptive to alternative ways of doing things without feeling criticized or threatened.'

Amongst his accomplishments at the Trust, Philip includes acting as a catalyst for a multidisciplinary review of budgeting and forecasting, which will lead to better resources allocation in the future. In addition, the Trust was beginning discussions with third parties in relation to PFI schemes for new hospitals, and Philip was able to bring his private sector experience to bear.

Gareth Cruddace was delighted with the work done by Sherwood: 'He brought a much more commercial approach to our business, gave an objective view of the financial health of the organization and provided quality assurance which showed that our internal team was pretty good. His input regarding the PFI negotiations was particularly valuable. Should the need arise, *I would most definitely employ interim managers in the future,*' he concluded.

Time management

Robert Townsend, former head of Avis, famously remarked about management consultants, 'They are people who borrow your watch to tell you what time it is and then walk off with it'.[5]

An interim manager, on the other hand, is someone who brings his own watch, sets yours by it, and leaves without a fuss when the alarm goes off.

TEN MYTHS ABOUT INTERIM MANAGERS

1 **Interim managers are redundant executives who can't get a proper job.** One of the UK's best-known interim agencies Executives on Assignments (EoA), reports that some 90 per cent of the interim managers on its database are former CEOs, senior managers or directors, in their last full-time jobs.

2 **Interim managers are loners, who don't work well in teams.** The reality is that interim managers require exceptional interpersonal skills if they are to function effectively in a line management position.

3 **Interim managers use assignments as a way to get a permanent job.** Some interims do accept full-time positions as a result of assignments, but a growing proportion are professional interims who prefer the alternative lifestyle. They are frequently offered full-time posts, but are typically overqualified for the job and refuse.

4 **Interim managers are desperate for work.** A large proportion of interim managers are financially secure and do it for the buzz.

5 Interim managers are glorified consultants. Although they are sometimes complementary, the two roles are very different. A consultant reports back to his or her firm, makes recommendations but never implements them, and is rarely judged on results. The interim manager, on the other hand, reports directly to the company's senior management, is responsible for implementing his own decisions, and lives or dies by his results.

6 Interim managers are expensive. Interim managers cost upwards of £400 per day. However, there are no hidden costs. The cost of employing a full-time senior manager, including company car, pension contributions, and other benefits such as holiday and sick pay, easily add up to much more than the interim. Also, interim managers have to be productive every day. They rarely attend conferences, training courses or get involved in other time consuming corporate activities such as interdepartmental meetings.

7 If interim managers are so good, why have so many been made redundant? Redundancy is no great respect of talent. Often, it affects those working in certain parts of a business, regardless of their competence. In many cases, too, voluntary redundancy succeeds in liberating the most entrepreneurial executives.

8 Interim managers are used to do the company's dirty work. They are used for a wide variety of assignments including close-downs, but also business start-ups and turnarounds. Many interim managers see one of their key roles as developing and nurturing less experienced managers. They get a buzz from developing people.

9 Interim managers are has-beens. It is true that interims have a few grey hairs. Most are in their 40s and 50s. The companies that use them see their experience as an advantage rather than a handicap.

10 **If interim management is such a good idea, why isn't it more widely used?** Research shows that the use of interim managers at senior levels has been growing at a rate of about 30 per cent year-on-year since the early 1990s. Yet, it remains largely misunderstood, partly for the reasons above.

NOTES TO CHAPTER 4

1 Coles, Margaret, 'Call Rent-a-boss for a quick fixer', *Sunday Times*, 18 February 1996.

2 Donkin, Richard, 'Managers reap an interim dividend', *Financial Times*, 28 May 1997.

3 Coles, Margaret, 'Call Rent-a-boss for a quick fixer', *Sunday Times*, 18 February 1996.

4 IMCOR, 1997.

5

Who makes a good interim manager?

The right stuff of interims

What skills are most in demand?

Interim managers vs executive temps

A special breed

Leaders

Money in the bank

Grey hairs

The interim mindset

Life after jobs

The boring bit about business life is when its all up and running and it's nice and smooth and all you are doing is just sort of caretaking it. I like the challenge of sorting things out, getting in there and making change and that's what you get from interim management.

PAUL BARTON, interim manager

One of the most important, and most misunderstood, aspects of interim management is that it takes a special sort of individual to fulfil the role. Some people give the impression that anyone who has ever held a management post could be a candidate for interim management. This simply isn't true.

'Some companies doubt whether an outsider can get immediate results in an unfamiliar environment. It is much harder to be a good interim manager than simply a good manager', Lucy Kellaway observed in the *Financial Times* in 1993.[1]

John Murray at PA Consulting agrees: 'That is the irony. Many of the available people are not good enough and the remainder are being fought over by the interim profession and the top management consultants.'

> *Experience and an outstanding track record are essential for an interim manager.*

THE RIGHT STUFF OF INTERIMS

The experts say that experience and an outstanding track record are essential for an interim manager. They also agree that motivation and life circumstances play an important part. To perform the role effectively requires an independence of thought and action that is different to that of a permanent employee who is concerned about keeping his job. The interim manager has a different agenda – one that assumes he will be moving on as soon as the task has been completed. He is self-reliant.

The profile of interim managers in Europe is broadly similar to that in the United States. A few years back, a report on the American 'head-renting market'[2] described them as: 'Pre-screened high level professionals, often earning more than $100 000 and no longer saddled with a stigma about temporary work.'

Most successful interims, it said, fall into one of the following broad classifications:

- independent consultants who use interim management firms as one of the channels through which they market their services.
- recycled retirees
- 'golden parachuters' (a term for people who have been given a large enough redundancy package to free them from the need to earn a regular income)
- lifestyle seekers, who want to exchange autonomy and the chance to pick assignments that interest them for the corporate rat race
- top-notch specialists, for whose talents there is unlikely to be enough consistent demand in any one firm to merit a permanent position, but for which there is market spread across an industry sector.

Management journalist Godfrey Golzen has written widely on the topic. He notes: 'The calibre of the people who become interim managers is far higher than that which is associated in most managers' minds with the idea of the "temp".'

According to Golzen,[3] interim managers fall into three principal categories:

- mid-career executives, either general managers or functional/technical specialists, who have decided to go out on their own as independent consultants
- new-age executives in their mid-30s or early 40s who, for family or lifestyle reasons, no longer want to be tied to corporate careers
- early retired senior managers who still want to play an active, if not a full-time, business role.

Whatever the circumstances or motivations of the interim manager, however, the role also requires a special set of skills and attributes. More than any other role, the interim must be able to walk into a new company and make things happen. He must be able to:

- inspire confidence and radiate credibility
- assimilate culture and context very quickly
- analyse what needs to be done and create an achievable plan
- 'fire up' an often demoralized workforce
- get things moving quickly
- side-step internal politics
- deliver on time and in budget
- make a clean exit.

So what are the attributes of a good interim manager? According to Martin Wood of Boyden Interim Executive: 'They must have the skills of a good consultant, and must be able to handle a team. They must not be politicians but must wear their hearts on their sleeves.'

Richard Foot at PA Consulting Group agrees that interims require special attributes. He warns that interim management is a tough and demanding proposition to which only a relatively small group of managers is suited. This, he says, has not always been widely understood. PA has done some ground-breaking research to build a profile of the successful interim (*see* Appendix A).

'They need maturity, stature, charisma, strength of personality and leadership', he says. 'This is not a role for the less experienced manager.'[4]

WHAT SKILLS ARE MOST IN DEMAND?

What research has been done in this area suggests that the range of skills and experience companies want from interim managers is as wide as the variety of assignments they are asked to manage.

For example, the MORI survey commissioned by Boyden found that the main role for which interim executives are recruited is finance director, followed by sales and marketing director and IT director. The most widely quoted reason for bringing in an interim executive is following the sudden departure of a key executive, or to take responsibility for a particular project such as integrating a new acquisition, preparing a subsidiary for disposal, or improving performance.

They need maturity, stature, charisma, strength of personality and leadership.

A survey carried out by the interim management agency GMS in 1997,[5] included a breakdown of their functional specialisms. It was based on a survey of some 700 interim managers. The findings suggest that interim managers are typically very capable people with experience at board or senior management level. The survey found the breakdown of disciplines among the respondents shown in Table 5.1.

Table 5.1   Breakdown of disciplines

Function	Percentage
Finance	20
General management	25
Sales and marketing	15
Production/ engineering	14
Purchasing/ distribution	3
IT	7
Human Resources	9
Other	7
	(Total 100)

That said, it should be stressed that interim managers are very rarely hired purely for a single functional skill. One of the pre-requisites of the interim role is a solid background in general management, and frequently international experience. Often, this is enhanced by a depth of knowledge and experience in a particular specialism such as finance or IT, but it is rarely an either/or situation.

In fact, many of those involved with interim management would say that an assignment that required only functional knowledge and experience was not really an interim management at all, but a variation on contracting. They would argue that the role of a true interim manager involves managing wider issues than simply the technical side.

So, if you want someone to install a new computer system, then get in a high level IT contractor. But if you want someone to manage the implementation of an IT solution, including overcoming middle management resistance, the buy-in of staff, delivery on time and within budget, the achievement of projected cost savings and other strategic objectives, then use an interim manager.

INTERIM MANAGERS vs EXECUTIVE TEMPS

The last point raises a bone of contention within the interim management world. At present, there are varying opinions about what exactly constitutes an interim assignment and what should more accurately be regarded as contracting or some other type of employment arrangement.

This confusion, some believe, has held back interim management from making the impact on corporate resourcing that it is capable of.

One of the most outspoken commentators on this issue in the

UK is Martin Wood, head of the interim management arm of headhunter Boyden International. He believes there are two distinct services currently being marketed as interim management.

'To accelerate the proven use of top-level interim executives, clients must understand the service they are buying. Two distinct and very different services are being offered under the same title of interim management.'

Referring to the findings from the 1997 MORI survey, he says: 'About 40 per cent of respondents understood the term to mean a high level resourcing option where implementation of change at or near board level is a prerequisite of the role. However, less than 10 per cent of all respondents had actually used it this way.

'Unfortunately, there has been liberal use of the term as an alternative title for upmarket "executive temping" where the executive is put in place to "hold the fort" or "keep the seat warm". This has hindered its strategic application as a real alternative to traditional management consultancy and demeaned its true worth.'

David Davies, an experienced interim agrees: 'Interim management is a niche market, not to be confused with executive temping or contract management. It will grow because after downsizing many companies are stretched and will need experienced executives for short-term assignments to cope with peaks and troughs, solve problems, and implement solutions.'[6]

After 16 years as finance director with high-tech companies including Toshiba, Davies who trained with Price Waterhouse as a chartered accountant and worked for Andersen Consulting, believes the interim role is a demanding one. 'You've got to have lots of hands-on experience, be able to stand back and take a strategic view, and be prepared to work for 12 hours a day. It's not for people planning early retirement.'

Wood adds: 'Proven interim executives are a small select

group numbering a few hundred only in the UK. They can operate comfortably and effectively in a wide range of sectors and businesses and are only as good as their last assignment. The long-term accelerated use of interim executive management as a top-level resourcing option will be critically dependent on the accurate matching of these few hundred against well-understood assignment briefs.'

> *You've got to have lots of hands-on experience.*

A SPECIAL BREED

Given the fall-out from downsizing and other corporate restructuring exercises in recent years, it is not surprising that the job market is awash with 'experienced managers'. Given the excitement and daily rates that interim managers command, it is not surprising either that many of these people would like to get in on the action. The reality is, however, that only a small percentage of these managers have the qualities required to be effective interim managers.

'Interims are a special breed', says Martin Wood. 'It would be unfair to pretend that any one can perform this role. They tend to be older, but probably 95 per cent of the grey hairs aren't suited to the job. The people we look for are the change agents.'

They also require a different set of skills to consultants. Whereas consultants typically advise the internal client, an interim must be able to walk into the office on day 1 and take charge. Success depends on being able to plug themselves into the company's culture and make the internal machinery work for them.

In his 1992 book on the subject,[7] Godfrey Golzen provided a list of personal traits of successful interim managers identified by the interim specialist Executive Interim Management (EIM).

That list remains as relevant today as it was when it was first published. It includes:

- wide management experience in relevant industries, from a generalist, not purely technical standpoint
- a sound management track record which inspires confidence with permanent employees on site
- strong analytical and communication skills
- the ability to size-up complex problems rapidly and to identify a course of action
- the ability to combine long-term strategic thinking with a keen sense of the importance of measurable results and of getting things done in the short term.
- being a focused, task-oriented achiever
- giving consistent leadership, combined with flexibility in reacting to events and circumstances when required
- the capacity to transfer knowledge to the permanent workforce at every level
- interpersonal and motivating skills
- awareness of political issues, in the corporate sense, coupled with the ability to take a detached view of them
- physical and mental toughness
- sufficient personal financial stability to be able to take tough decisions without fear of the assignment being terminated for that reason
- a strong sense of autonomy and independence – although loners do not make good interim managers. Successful interim managers are not dependent on popular approval or externally conferred marks of status.

Talking to interims themselves, certain common attitudes emerge. There seem to be a number of additional qualities that are shared by those who are effective in the role. These include:

- a bias for action

- an ability to think both tactically and strategically, and to know the difference
- being overqualified for the role
- possessing excellent interpersonal skills
- a natural bias towards change (change agents rather than status quo managers)
- mobility (75 per cent of assignments involve temporary relocation)[8]
- a few grey hairs
- professional restlessness.

Where do interims come from?

According to GMS, interim managers come into the market from a wide variety of backgrounds and personal circumstances.[9]

- Some are full-time, self-employed independent consultants.
- Some are full-time consultants within an established consultancy but who are hired out individually.
- Some have taken early retirement.
- Some are between jobs and are looking for a suitable executive appointment. (The concern that this may limit commitment, says GMS, is a real one that it takes great care to assess.)
- Some, because of personal circumstances, do not want a long-term commitment or a full-time commitment.
- Some prefer project-based work that offers both a fair reward for their skills and expertise and time for other personal activities between assignments.

What is perhaps most revealing of all about GMS's research, however, is the finding that 30 per cent of all executives becoming independents do so because they want to be independent. Another 30 per cent attribute the reason to 'other push factors', whilst 34 per cent quote redundancy as the reason.

LEADERS

A key strength of interim managers is their ability to achieve objectives by working with the existing staff. This requires exceptional interpersonal skills and leadership qualities. One US interim network describes the benefits of the interim role simply as 'the ability to get things done through people'.[10]

Interim managers, it says:

- quickly devise measurements
- create individual and departmental accountability
- re-prioritize and restructure job descriptions.

But above all they:

- re-recruit the services, minds and enthusiasm of the existing workforce at all levels.

The ability to lead, is crucial to the role. But, here again, there is some confusion about the sort of people who become interims. As PA Consulting's John Murray observes, 'There is a false premise in some quarters about interims that they are loners: They couldn't work in corporations because they were rotten managers so they got fired so now they "hire their gun out". This is not true. 'We feel very strongly that without above average leadership skills, you can't be an effective interim.

'At a very simple level we look at what I call eyeball skills; their body language, their willingness to share thinking, the lucidity of their communication – all of those rather subtle indicators that here you have someone that people will follow. Of course, we always ask people to describe their leadership style. What do your subordinates think of you? What does your boss think of you, and how do you get motivated if you have a weak team and so on. Listening to those answers

> *Without above average leadership skills, you can't be an effective interim*

tells you whether they are leadership material or not – if they are, when they come in to a client they can raise the competency of the team.'

MONEY IN THE BANK

In Britain, research carried out by Russam GMS, indicates that 60 per cent of interims are aged between 45 and 55, and 38 per cent are between 48 and 53. Two-fifths of them took up interim management after being made redundant.

Charles Russam, head of Russam GMS, notes that, for the majority of interim managers, the change of career is triggered by redundancy or early retirement. Most, he says, have enough financial security that they don't require a steady income.

'They are probably used to a salary of between £40 000 and £50 000 and can make the same money on temporary assignments', he says. 'If the kids have grown up, and their partner has a job, a senior executive with some money in the bank may decide they don't want to be beholden to an employer again.'

It's a point echoed by PA Consulting's Stuart Cain: 'If someone has made some money or taken early retirement – that's good. You must be doing it for the satisfaction of doing the job not just for the money. The converse is true, if you're desperate for the money that can cause serious conflicts of interest. You have to be objective. You have to be commercially detached – doing it for the excitement and to put something back in. Interim managers are the sort of people who like fixing things.'

GREY HAIRS

One thing that interims do have in common is maturity. The role demands a level of experience not usually found in managers under the age of 40. Many interims are much older, in their 60s. As one interim notes: 'One of the great things about the role is that a few grey hairs are actually an asset.'

The role is very demanding, however, requiring a good level of physical fitness. Interims must be just about the only professionals who actually boast about their years. On their web page,[11] for example, managers from an interim firm based in Ohio, in America's Midwest, introduce themselves as follows:

> *Interim managers are the sort of people who like fixing things.*

'We're a cadre of chaos-tolerant, internetworked management ancients who've camped out at the cliff's edges since Sputnik. Along the way, we've found some techno-savvy upstarts, each with a good decade or more of industrial battle-hardening. On-call to answer your latest business challenges and help you dominate your market competition.'

And add:

'On the whole, we're a dispersed group of former corporate good-guys – now unleashed. A fluid amalgam of independent, yet collaborative professional problem-solvers.'

Their straight-talking promises are typical of interims. For example:

You'll find we're authentic. Not superhuman but aware and well grounded in creatively using and passing on sound fundamentals. You'll get hands-on leaders; leaders who help you produce other leaders, not just followers.'

'You'll get good, solid talent with expertise to do the job well and on time.'

'You won't pay for our learning curve. Most of our mistakes have long-since been paid for.'

'You won't overpay. We're not cheap, but we're fair. We'll cost justify ourselves with plenty of payback to you. No long-term contracts or significant fixed costs.'

'You'll see we're working for your stated results, not timesheet hours. We're there on site, hands-on, working beside you.'

At the same time, as companies become more aware of the seniority and experience of the interim management pool, the assignments they are being used for are becoming increasingly strategic in their nature. Where once they were seen as mere stop-gaps, increasingly they are called in as company doctors to improve performance or to put right corporate deficiencies.

This follows a trend already clear in the US, where interims are now an established feature of corporate life, and are often hired in for tasks such as turning round loss-making subsidiaries, reorganizing entire departments, or reducing corporate debt.

In effect, where an interim might once have been brought in as a safe pair of hands while a qualified replacement was found, they are also now being brought in as trouble-shooters, to sort out problems. This is increasingly reflected in the kudos that is associated with the role.

The fact that most are old enough to have some mistakes under their belt makes interims better value. As one former IT director in his 50s, explains: 'I've been doing what I do for a very long time. It may sound immodest but I'm very good at what I do. I've made every mistake possible. Part of my value to clients is that I never make the same mistake twice.'

> *Increasingly they are called in as company doctors.*

There are echoes here of the Allied general in the First World War who said he didn't want anyone on his staff who hadn't experienced failure or retreat. There is something reassuring, too, about any sign that companies are reassessing the value of experience.

Archie Dalton

Archie Dalton was a an interim manager for 7 years before his appointment as chairman and major shareholder of Shaw Carpets Ltd, a £25 million turnover business. This opportunity arose as a result of an interim management assignment through NBS Interim Management, part of the NBS recruitment group and one of the UK's leading interim intermediaries.

Commenting on the challenges of interim management, he says: 'Clearly, you must have a wealth of industrial experience as well as the ability to make things happen, create change and overcome the resistance to change which can be found in organizations.

'In essence, you must offer clear leadership; have the ability to communicate your knowledge; be adaptive; have high personal energy and drive; and the ability to motivate.'

THE INTERIM MINDSET

The successful interim managers we spoke to also seem to have something else; something intangible and very difficult to describe. It has something to do with the way they think about work and jobs. More than just an attitude, it's as if they have made the switch to a new set of mental software about the world of careers. This enables them to place the interim role in context.

Many commentators claim that, at this point in our employment history, we are in a state of flux. One way to think about it is to regard the current state of affairs as part of a transition from the old world of 'jobs for life' to the new world of 'portfolio careers'.

In trying to understand and come to terms with these changes, many of us owe a huge debt to the ideas of Charles Handy, who perhaps more than any other, has tried to make sense and reassure people about what for many of them is a frightening transition. It is in this context that interim management must be viewed. Those who make the mental leap are the ones most likely to succeed in the role.

We are now a good deal further along this learning curve than we were even 5 years ago. Today, for example, attitudes about work have undergone a significant shift. Interim managers seem much further round this curve than most of us.

For several years in the early 1990s, one of the authors edited a column in *The Times* devoted to the plight of readers who suddenly found themselves redundant. The 'Life After Redundancy' column was a reaction to the first recession to really hit white-collar workers as hard as blue-collar workers. Suddenly, many middle-class people in their mid-50s with comfortable incomes, large mortgages and private school fees to pay found themselves out of work. It gradually dawned on them that they would not find another full-time position.

To judge by the letters the column received, many of these people were taken entirely by surprise. Until the axe fell on them, they had no idea that the rules of the career game had changed. Today, thankfully, that is no longer the case. We have moved on.

Today, most people are aware that jobs for life are a thing of the past. Indeed, survey after survey shows that those who are currently working for employers expect to lose their job or change employers at least once. Interim managers have embraced this change. Many say they are relieved to be in control of their own destinies.

According to John A. Thompson, CEO of the US interim firm IMCOR and the author of 'The Portable Executive', all of us should now be adopting what he calls the 'portable mindset'.

'At all levels, organizations are developing relationships with their managers that bring with them a set of different expectations relating to the workforce. Organizations are asking their managers to develop a portable mindset.'[12]

To do so, Thompson argues, they need to develop the following philosophies, which mirror those of the interim manager:

- View themselves as a business; their product as their skills, abilities and experience; and see their employer as a 'client'.
- Understand that rather than holding an open-ended job, their role is to uncover specific functional goals and to provide specific deliverables. These might include developing cost and process savings or acquiring or providing specific skills.
- Recognize the value of self-motivated learning and training that keeps skills and knowledge at state-of-the-art levels.
- Understand that a specific organization with its changing intellectual capital requirements may only need them for a short time, but that numerous other organizations will also need them for a time.
- Therefore, don't expect the organization to provide 'lifetime positions' but be prepared to constantly seek out new market opportunities.
- Remain focused on results. Past accomplishments influence future employability.

LIFE AFTER JOBS

The generations that follow will not know any employment other than the new world of work. Recent research[13] already confirms that the young managers of today have a very different view of careers to previous generations. An understanding of how they see the new world of work is instructive. (After all, this is the same world that we must now adapt to.)

Jay A. Conger, a former visiting professor at Harvard and INSEAD, and now at the University of Southern California, has carried out extensive interviews with managers from successive generations. His work confirms a significant shift in attitudes.

> *Don't expect the organization to provide 'lifetime positions'.*

According to Professor Conger, the Silent Generation – composed of those born between 1925 and 1942 – was filled with the children of those who went through the Great Depression of the 1930s. They were influenced by their parents' hardships to value job security. The term 'Company Man' was invented for this generation; they were the managers of the 1950s through to the 1970s.

Then came the Baby Boomers. Born between 1942 and 1963; they grew into the Yuppies of the 1980s. Their rebellious attitude was influenced in America by Vietnam and Watergate, which taught them to distrust authority.

Following the Baby Boomers are the Gen Xers. The product of dual-career families and record divorce rates, they are better educated than their predecessors, and want to judge – and be judged – on merit rather than on status.

The Gen Xers share the Baby Boomers' distrust of hierarchy, preferring more informal arrangements. They are also far less loyal to their companies than previous generations. According to Professor Conger, the contract of lifetime employment which began to deteriorate for the Baby Boomers, feels practically non-existent for the Gen Xers.

This is having an impact on companies. As John Murray from PA Consulting Group notes: 'Thirty years ago, the top gradu-ates in this country either went into the civil service, or they joined large international companies, such as Shell, ICI, BP, Unilever. These days, those companies have become much less interesting to graduates. Now who is interesting? The big con-sultancies who are offering fascinating careers working for 20 Unilevers instead of just one.

'So, instead of climbing up a single corporate ladder and becoming a co-ordinator at Shell aged 50 and taking out a retirement at 58 as a director, these people are making seven fig-ure salaries in many cases by the time they are 40. Investment banking, that's even bigger money. So, there is increased star-vation of the big manufacturers by the seduction of the service providers. Big problem. They get it back by the way, because the consultants come and advise them, but it costs a lot more.'

The alternative, is to use an interim manager.

The New Career Rules

Bruce Tulgan has written about his generation – so-called Generation X – and its attitude towards work. In a 'memorandum to the workforce of the future', he offers a new career manifesto for the 'post job era'.[14] (It could equally be the interim manager's manifesto.)

'It's all over', he says. 'All of it. Not just job security. Jobs are all over. We have entered the post jobs era and there's no turning back.'

Generation Xers are realists. As far as they are concerned, traditional jobs are something their fathers and mothers had. They are from another era.

Tulgan examines how those attitudes play against changes taking place within companies. Their early experience of corporate life was the pain of downsizing. They witnessed the redundancies of the early 1990s. For them, jobs are transitory, and the old career ladder is defunct.

This is something Gen Xers can take in their stride. 'While none of us will have a "job", in the old-fashioned sense, there is still a lot of work to be done', Tulgan writes. 'Stop thinking about getting and keeping a good job. Make a list of everything you can do that someone might want to pay you for. Sell your most valuable talents on the open market.'

In place of the traditional career ladder, he offers 'five essential ingredients of the re-invented career'. The new rules are:

- **Learn voraciously:** the next generation of employees already has an insatiable appetite for information. This means: creating their own opportunities to learn; taking control of their post-school education; maximizing all corporate training opportunities; and turning job-hopping into a personal training programme.

▶

● **Concentrate on relationships:** relationships with individuals will be the most reliable institutions in the post-job era. 'Identify and seek out the real decision makers; turn every contract into a multiple contract; identify and win over gate-keepers; get on the right persons radar "then prove that you are more than just a blip"; take personal responsibility for keeping relationships fizzing.'

● **Add value continuously:** the most successful workers today are chameleon-like day-to-day value-adders.

● **Be balanced:** set clear priorities in working and personal lives, and then live by them no matter what. Personal values and well-being are vital to career success.

● **Take it one year at a time:** in a changing environment long-term goals are good, but long-term planning is useless. Young people today, he suggests, should plan their lives – and careers – one year at a time.

CASE STUDY

Automating the British Library – project implementation

When the British Library first began to think about the most ambitious project in its history – moving to a new location – automating its referencing systems was critical to the planning process.

One of the objectives of creating a new home for the British Library was to encourage a wider audience. The project to automate the system has helped to ensure this objective was met. An interim manager was brought in to project manage. Since opening on 24 November 1997 at its new Bloomsbury site near St Pancras, the British Library has already handled more than a quarter of a million enquiries.

In many ways, automating a brand new, purpose-built site was the easy part. The building is designed with under-floor cabling throughout, units specifically designed to take desktop monitors and the space to install a mechanical book handling system.

Readers have access to the huge collection, which ranges from 4000 year-old tree bark to 250 000 new items which are added each year, via several new computer systems.

Most of the library's collection, which has been developed over the last 250 years and exceeds 150 million separate items, will be relocated from the present 20 sites, including the British Museum in Bloomsbury, to the new site at St Pancras over the next 2 years.

Once installed in the basement book storage areas, each item is recorded on the new database. This allows readers to access items for research from a computer terminal, and each item is able to be tracked wherever it is in the building.

The challenge was obtaining the appropriate project-management skills to ensure that an IT project of this scale and importance was achieved successfully.

For the British Library, the basic criteria for the interim IT implementation manager were clear:

● the ability to identify the appropriate technology
● and access to a skilled resource to develop and install it.

Add to this an ability to handle a large project and to influence at the highest level within the organization and the description was almost complete. The final attribute, which was more of a nice to have, than a requirement, was hands-on experience of automating libraries.

Eric Mason, a senior IT consultant with wide-ranging experience of managing large IT installations including P & O, Euro Disney, First Choice Holidays, and Thomas Cook, was selected for the assignment.

Mason spent 10 years at Digital Equipment Corporation (DEC), latterly as IT director and had just completed an 18-month spell at the London Borough of Lambeth, managing the project to procure and implement a library archive and reference system, when he was approached about the assignment at the British Library.

With direct and recent experience of a library system, he had an obvious advantage. (The reality in interim management is that there is no time or space for a learning curve. The priority for clients is that the managers actively contribute from day one.)

As John Mahoney, IS Director of the British Library explains: 'A project of this size and importance required a number of specialist project managers to help it succeed. The skill is in the combined strength of management which existed between those within the library team and the external managers who were able to bring experience of similar situations and proven solutions to the problems we encountered.'

The automation project required the combined expertise of the internal team, which included librarians and technical experts, external consultants and software developers. Four separate, but linked automated systems, lie at the heart of the improved service for readers.

The On-line Public Access Catalogue (OPAC) will hold over 12 million records by the time St Pancras is fully operational. The software was developed specifically for the new site. It is a large, complex database which is easily expandable. The Digital Alpha servers that were chosen to run the system provide it with a high degree of flexibility and an excellent response time.

The Automated Book Request System verifies availability of the publications required, prints the request in the storage area, tracks and communicates progress of the publication from the storage area to the reader. The system has been developed to provide the most secure method of tracking the range of materials available to readers while at the same time allowing for complete flexibility.

The Mechanical Bookhandling system routes the container to the correct collection point.

Three hundred computer terminals have been installed to provide readers with the ability to browse through the catalogues and order books. The system manages all the reader records and the vast inventory of material held over the library's seven sites.

The technology consists of two Digital Vax servers and three Digital Alpha servers running a 40 Gbyte database with 300 Pentium PC's over a Cisco ATM fibre optic network. Over the next 18 months the

PC client population is expected to grow to nearly 500. Since the opening, an additional 170 terminals have been added to the network.

Interim manager, Eric Mason is currently involved with the implementation of Phase II of the 'biggest book move in history'. The rare books reading room was opened in March 1998, Music will open in May and Maps, Indian and Oriental will follow, with Science and Manuscripts opening early in 1999. The public galleries are open 7 days a week for access to Dickens and Shakespeare amongst others.

NOTES TO CHAPTER 5

1 Kellaway, Lucy, 'Troubleshooters for hire', *Financial Times*, 9 August 1993.
2 *Consultants News*, Issue 3, Winter 1989.
3 Golzen, Godfrey, *Interim Management: A new dimension in corporate performance*, Kogan Page, 1992.
4 Houlder, Vanessa, 'When even the boss is a temp', *Financial Times*, 11 August 1997.
5 'The GMS Guide to Interim Management', 1997.
6 Altman, Wilf, 'Pressures of a portfolio lifestyle', *Evening Standard*, 19 May 1998.
7 Golzen, Godfrey, *Interim Management*, Kogan Page, 1992.
8 Forbes.
9 'The GMS Guide to Interim Management', GMS, 1995.
10 Frequently asked questions and concerns about interim professional management, Temporary Executives – Business Turnaround Artists, Ohio, USA.
11 Frequently asked questions and concerns about interim professional management, Temporary Executives – Business Turnaround Artists, Ohio, USA.
12 Thompson, John A., 'The portable purchasing and supply manager', *Purchasing Today*, February 1998.
13 Tulgan, Bruce, *Work This Way*, Capstone, 1998.
14 Tulgan, Bruce, *Work this Way*, Capstone, 1998.

Marketing yourself as an interim manager

The specialists

Why use an intermediary?

Choosing and marketing yourself to an intermediary

What qualities does an intermediary look for?

What should you expect from an intermediary?

There is work out there if we were able to turn ourselves into tiny independent businesses – 'portfolio people' I call them, with a portfolio of clients and products. The trouble is that we prepared ourselves for a world of jobs not customers. As independents, we don't know what to sell or how to sell it, even how to price it or make out an invoice. We shall have to learn.

CHARLES HANDY, *Beyond Certainty*

Some interims market themselves directly to potential clients. Typically, this involves mailing a detailed CV and covering letter, but some go much further. For example, after winning a number of interim assignments, Richard McKeown, a chartered company secretary, spends £5000 a year on marketing himself. This includes employing a public relations expert.[1] He produces a glossy brochure, marketing his skills, experience, and previous assignments. He is, in his own words, 'the all-singing, all-dancing one-man band'.

Most interims use a combination of their own marketing skills and registering with specialist interim firms to find assignments. It is a logical response to an occupational hazard that faces all interim managers: how do you find your next assignment when you're working flat out on the current one? The answer, in most cases, is to let the specialists find it for you.

> *Some interims market themselves directly to potential clients.*

THE SPECIALISTS

The growth of interim management has been accompanied by the growth of specialist firms operating within the recruitment sector. These firms, many of them offshoots of existing recruitment firms, provide an important service to both clients and individual interim managers. They act as intermediaries, matching individuals from their pool or database of active interims with the requirements of particular assignments. In this regard, they provide a clearing house for the dynamic and growing interim market.

'One way to think of us is as a theatrical agency with a drawer full of actors and a handful of roles', says PA Consulting's John Murray. 'Interims work in a linear mode, one assignment at a time. We can do their marketing for them.'

The origins and approach of these intermediaries reflect the diversity of the recruitment sector. So, for example, at the top end of the market are interim firms which specialize in filling interim assignments at board level or just below. Others, however, are broader churches, covering assignments at middle management level as well. As one might expect, there is strong competition between the various intermediaries and the usual war of words about who provides the highest calibre managers and the most comprehensive service.

Given the nature of the work carried out by these specialist interim intermediaries, it is no surprise that a number of them are offshoots of executive search firms, or headhunters as they are more commonly known. Others are familiar names from the world of management consultancy which have well-established executive recruitment operations. Still others operate in a way that is closer to the recruitment agency approach, with a much larger database of interim managers ranging from director to functional manager to draw from.

Some of these firms have been in the market longer than others, and have therefore built up their expertise over a longer period. One of the oldest interim specialists in Europe, for example, is EIM (Executive Interim Management), which traces it origins back to Holland in the late-1970s, where it operated as BCG Interim Management.[2] EIM is 51 per cent owned by Egon Zehnder, one of Europe's leading headhunters. Today, EIM has offices in a number of European countries as well as Australia, and has recently opened an office in New York. Other leading interim specialists on the European mainland include the Swiss firms Adia and Brainforce.

In the UK, where the interim market is believed to be growing at an annual rate of between 20 and 30 per cent, there are a number of well-established intermediaries, which, via their parent organizations, are part of international networks. These include PA Consulting Group's Global Interim Management Practice division (part of PA Consulting), Protem (set up by headhunters Heidrick & Struggles), Boyden Interim Executive (part of the US headhunter Boyden International), and NBS Interim Management, part of the Norman Broadbent Search and Selection group.

Other interim intermediaries tend to be more national, or regional, in their orientation. Russam GMS for example has a number of offices around the UK, Albermarle is a subsidiary of a well-known search and selection firm, and Barton Interim Management grew out of an executive search firm in the West of England and which continues to primarily serve that region.

There are also some new players entering the market, offering even more specialized services. Rent-an-MBA, for example has only Master of Business Administration graduates on its books, and is backed by the Association of MBAs. Another recent innovation involves the provision of interim company secretaries to help companies cope with extra workload, for example, during mergers and acquisitions.[3]

In the US, where the interim concept has been diluted by a plethora of terms including 'head renting' and 'executive leasing', there are even more variations on the intermediary role. There are many more independent consultants who take on interim assignments to augment their consultancy work, and who use the intermediaries for different purposes.

One estimate in the early 1990s, put the number of firms in the US involved in interim management at 30.[4] Today, the number claiming to be interim specialists is much higher.

What is also clear is that, as the interim market grows, intermediaries are developing and operating in different ways.

Some of those firms at the top end of the market such as EIM, for example, take responsibility for the work that is carried out by the interims they place. The extent to which different firms stay in touch and support their interims in the field also varies.

PA Consulting believes that an essential part of its role is to support the interim executive throughout the assignment. Others, however, see their role simply as matching interim managers on their books with assignments. They prefer to let the interim manager get on with it.

As is to be expected in a competitive market, there is the usual posturing among intermediaries about which approach offers the best solution for a client looking to fill an assignment. Some interim firms, for example, behave much more like middlemen or traditional recruitment agencies providing a list of possible candidates. Others regard themselves as a professional matching service, much more akin to headhunters.

The critical issue for the would-be interim is deciding which service best meets your needs. The more senior you are, the more likely you are to benefit from talking to the intermediaries that operate at the top end of the interim market. The blanket use of the term interim management to describe different sorts of service, however, can be confusing. Martin Wood of Boyden Interim Executive agrees:

'Interim management is in need of sectorizing', he says.[5] At mid-management level, the success of a recruitment firm hinges on having a database of thousands and being able to give clients half a dozen CVs to choose from. But, at senior levels, Wood maintains, his clients are offered one or at most two interims who are best matched to the job.

'For a top level job there are perhaps only three interims in the country who can do it, and only one is likely to be available', he says.

The approach of EIM, which also operates at the top end of the market, is to determine the goals and limits of an assignment, then match them with the single best candidate for the job. It does not go in for so-called 'beauty contests' in which the client company chooses from several candidates.

The interim process

The Connecticut-based interim firm IMCOR describes the interim process as follows.

IMCOR places executives as project leaders and contract line managers who:
- earn a minimum annual base compensation of US $80 000
- have at least 10 years of management experience
- possess a high level of industry and functional knowledge.

IMCOR assignments:
- can range from 3 months to 2 years, typically lasting 6 months
- are in all functions and industries.
- are at all sizes of national and international companies, ranging from new ventures to Fortune 100 companies.

The interim process – IMCOR:
- works with clients to define an assignment, its objectives and duration
- moves rapidly to source and present candidates, often within days
- participates in the client/ candidate interview process.
- puts executives onto IMCOR's payroll, while they work for the client company
- charges the client company, not the executive, a monthly assignment fee.

▶

Some firms also impose a stiff penalty on companies that want to hire its interims on a permanent basis, as they prefer to keep them available for future assignments.

In some ways, this is less of a problem for the wily interim manager, as there is nothing to stop him or her from being on the books of several different interims firms at the same time. Indeed playing the field is often the best strategy.

Rent-an-MBA

Started in London in 1993 by founder Patrick O' Conner, Rent-an-MBA is a specialist firm catering for specific, short-term business needs, and for highly qualified executives with too little work. It operates on the interim management principle, with one distinguishing difference – all the executives have a Master of Business Administration (MBA) degree.

O'Conner was surprised to find so many MBA graduates available for contract work. 'I was amazed at their quality', he says. 'Yet a lot had fallen out of companies and were not so much unemployed as under employed.'

The contract between employer and employee is so unsafe, he says, that many MBAs are taking the initiative and rather than cling to unreliable jobs are choosing to manage their own career by planning a 'portfolio existence'.

Rent-an-MBA has the backing of the UK's Association of MBAs. It offers a rapid matching service with its 500 plus pool of MBAs and client needs. Speed can be vital. In one case, a call came through requesting an American MBA to handle a tough assignment in international human resources in the US. Within 3 hours it was arranged – at nine the next morning, the MBA reported to the company for an interview. A few days later he flew to America.[6]

WHY USE AN INTERMEDIARY?

A cynic might ask why use an intermediary at all? Why not cut out the middleman? From the point of view of both individual interim managers and client companies, however, intermediaries provide a number of valuable functions.

> *Playing the field is often the best strategy.*

'Both companies and individuals can get their fingers very badly burned in the interim field', warns PA Consulting's John Murray. 'We provide the added value of risk minimization through our selection procedure. We take the references and we do the eyeballing – we've got a feel for this market by now. It's a bit like trading horse flesh and we know how to look at the teeth and pick at the hooves.

'We know the sort of problems that plague interims and how to deal with them. We understand their independence of spirit and how that finds expression in their work. How you manage around it and, of course, we can give clients a choice in a very short period of time.'

Even though the individual intermediaries may have different approaches, there are some basic services they all provide. In one key area, interim management firms are more akin to employment agencies than to head-

> *It's a bit like trading horse flesh.*

hunters. Interim intermediaries take a percentage of the daily fee the client pays for the services of the interim managers. In general, interim firms charge between 25 and 30 per cent of the total fee income. This level of charge, they say, is justified by the following benefits and services which they provide:

Key benefits to the individual are:

- marketing
- reputation and credibility in the market

- matching to assignments
- fee negotiation
- security of payment (especially important when the client company is in trouble)
- briefing and preparing for interview
- induction
- support (someone to talk to/shoulder to cry on)
- legal advice
- contingency planning
- networking opportunities
- arbitration.

Marketing

This is without doubt one of the most useful functions the intermediary performs. The fact is that, when you are involved in a very demanding assignment, there is little time to market yourself to other potential clients, or to line up your next job. A good intermediary, however, will be in regular contact and will know when you are likely to be available for your next assignment. In this way, they will be constantly marketing your skills and experience in the marketplace.

Some interim managers do market themselves to potential clients as well as signing on with intermediaries. But the vast majority prefer to concentrate their personal marketing efforts at the interview stage.

But, there is another side to this issue. Not every manager has a background in marketing, and even those who do often find it harder to market themselves than a product or service. The truth is that it's often more effective to let someone else sing your praises than it is to do it yourself. The interim expert should know the market and therefore how to position an individual to their best advantage. The interim specialist is also usually better placed to discuss any concerns, and does so in strict confidence.

Reputation and credibility in the market

A reputable interim firm will have much greater credibility with clients than individual as yet 'unknown' interim manager. Clients seeking interim managers prefer to go to a specialist provider, who can usually match their requirements from its pool of executives, rather than contacting several individual interims on the off-chance that one of them is available.

Clients rely on the professionalism of the interim specialist to match the interim with the assignment. In many cases, the client will have already used the services of the interim firm and have established a good relationship based on trust. By the same token, an interim intermediary

> *Clients prefer to go to a specialist provider.*

that's in the market for the long term knows the importance of repeat business. In many cases, endorsements from satisfied clients are the interim firm's best marketing tool.

Moreover, an introduction from a tried and tested intermediary provides instant credibility for a manager looking for his first interim assignment. Interim firms live or die by their reputation. The good ones guard it jealously.

Matching to assignments

It is the job of the intermediary to match the client's requirements with the right interim manager. For this purpose, interim firms keep a database of active interim managers. They will also know if a suitable candidate registered with them is nearing the end of an assignment and is on the look out for the next position.

Once a shortlist has been prepared and presented to the client, the intermediary will then make the appropriate introductions, creating an opportunity for both sides to make an assessment of each other. According to PA's Stuart Cain, it is often not so much about technical matching of skills as chemistry matching. Many different issues will come into that decision, including the culture of the host company and the personality and leadership style of the interim candidate.

Briefing and interview

An integral part of the introduction process is a detailed briefing. Typically, the intermediary will first have to generate a detailed brief based on the client's requirements, This is often a skill in itself, involving a high level of expertise to tease out the real issues.

On the whole, clients that have used interims before are much clearer about what the assignment involves. Those trying it for the first time, however, typically have to go through a learning curve (it is an important part of the intermediary's role to help them through that process). Once the client brief is clear, the shortlisted interim managers can be briefed.

Fee negotiation

One of the most important roles performed by the intermediary, of course, is to negotiate the best fee. There are two important points here. One is that the specialist should know the going rate for a manager's expertise. Someone who spends his or her time exclusively dealing with interims, after all, should have a better understanding of the prevailing market conditions than someone who dips a toe in every six months or so.

> The intermediary will first have to generate a detailed brief.

In many circumstances, too, the intermediary will know how urgent the assignment is, how much is at stake, and even the negotiating style and culture of the client – all aspects that the individual interim cannot hope to have prior knowledge of. The interim firm will also know which skills or expertise are in short supply among interims at any particular time, ensuring that those who have those skills are properly rewarded.

An obvious example here is that, in the months leading up to 2000, IT managers with experience of leading projects to tackle the Millenium problem are likely to be in great demand. (Knowing this, a number of former IT directors say they are planning to postpone their retirement and work as interim managers until 2000.) As the Millenium time bomb ticks on, too, the interim specialist is best placed to negotiate their fees.

It is true, of course, that the intermediary is also concerned to offer a fair price to clients. This has the advantage from the interim's point of view of preventing them from being 'over sold', so that they are unable to deliver on the promises made on their behalf. So, why should the intermediary get the best fee for you? Remember, he works on a percentage basis: the bigger the fee, the bigger his cut.

Security of payment

Another important service provided by intermediaries is debt collection. Most reputable interim firms guarantee the interim manager's fee, regardless. Not only does this remove the irksome task of the administration so that you can concentrate on the task in hand, it also ensures the interim manager does not become embroiled in disputes over money.

In certain situations, too, it ensures that the interim gets paid whatever the outcome of the assignment. Take the case of a turnaround situation or a close down, for example, where there is a risk that the patient will not respond to the treatment. In such cases, the interim knows that the financial arrangement is with the intermediary and not the ailing company. This provides a degree of added financial security.

Induction and clarification of reporting lines

Most intermediaries will help prepare the way for the interim by clarifying issues such as whether other employees should be told that the new appointment is an interim, reporting lines, and ensuring the necessary introduction and induction process is in place to enable the interim to be accepted into the culture of the company.

> Another important service provided by intermediaries is debt collection.

Support

Some intermediaries regard their role as over once the interim is in *situ*. The more professional ones, however, keep in regular contact with both interim and client. In this way they monitor progress, head off any problems, and generally keep tabs on how the assignment is going. They are also available to provide a sounding board or occasionally to console or sympathize with an interim who is finding it tough going.

Legal advice

Because of its relative newness, the contractual side of interim management is a potential minefield for the inexperienced. It is one of the intermediaries' primary roles to provide legal advice and a degree of contractual protection to both interim managers and the corporate clients. Where the professionals are unable to answer a query or resolve a legal issue themselves, they will usually have access to employment lawyers.

One other point is worth covering here – the matter of professional indemnity insurance. The position with professional indemnity insurance for interims is similar to that for consultants. In most cases, it is well worth investing in. Once again, the intermediary should be able to provide detailed assistance with this.

Contingency planning

One of the more subtle aspects of the intermediary's role is that of cipher. Interim firms who take their role seriously recognize that the client's brief may not be the whole story. In many cases, what the client says needs fixing is not what actually needs fixing. It is part of the intermediary's job to read between the lines, to interpret what is being said, and to brief the interim accordingly.

One rather romantic way to think of this is to regard the interim as the commando who is parachuted behind enemy lines to complete a mission. It is part of the job of those who send him to understand and brief him about the conditions he is likely to encounter on the ground – including the level of resistance and support from above.

One interim firm calls it 'second guessing' the way the project will go. It is often sensible to include some surplus capacity when assigning an interim.

'The nature of change management is that the situation will be different in 6 or 9 months time. We try to anticipate what could happen. So we'll put someone in of sufficient stature to handle what we can see could happen down the road. In other words, we try to put in an executive who can handle the assignment under scenario A, B or C.'

> Regard the interim as the commando who is parachuted behind enemy lines.

'Quite a lot of two-layer briefing goes on. What we're trying to ensure is that there is reserve there that can be drawn on if needed. There is redundancy in the structure, so if one spur fails them there is another to prop things up. A lot goes on beneath the surface.'

Networking opportunities

One of the downsides of being a professional interim manager is that there are few opportunities to meet kindred spirits. In most cases, when on an assignment the interim will be working in an environment which is predominately made up of permanent employees. Once the assignment ends, he or she returns to glorious isolation from the corporate world.

Recognizing this, some interim management firms provide opportunities for interims to meet up and network with one another.

PA Consulting, for example, hosts regular lunches for a dozen or so of its interim managers. These occasions allow those attending to compare notes and trade war stories, something that they seem to enjoy.

In future, it is likely that interims will create their own executive clubs and networks to provide this sort of support. Or, that intermediaries will seize on these sorts of activities as a means to add value to the relationship. Clients may also find it useful to discuss their interim experiences with clients from other companies. Such activities are sure to help establish interim management as a mainstream business solution and strategic resource.

Arbitration

In the event of a dispute or a communications breakdown between client and interim, it is also part of the intermediary's job to step in and arbitrate. What is actually surprising is how rare such problems are. This is a testament to the professionalism of those who become interim managers.

CHOOSING AND MARKETING YOURSELF TO AN INTERMEDIARY

To some extent, the intermediaries hold the key to obtaining the best assignments. It is therefore essential that the aspiring interim manager identify the right intermediary – or more likely intermediaries – and markets him or herself effectively to them.

Interim firms receive literally hundreds of telephone calls, letters and CVs from hopeful candidates. Many of those enquiries – probably the vast majority, in fact – will be from people who are unsuitable for the role. This is a simple fact of life in today's corporate world. There is just no room any more for passengers.

To some extent, business journalists have helped raise the hopes of displaced managers who are desperate to find a useful way to use their talents. We have done that, usually unintentionally, by writing articles which give the impression that interim management is an easy option. It isn't. It requires a special set of skills, which only a limited proportion of the management population possesses.

> *Intermediaries hold the key to obtaining the best assignments.*

In time, as the market for interims becomes more developed, it may well be possible to develop some of the necessary skills (through in-house development programmes which are part of a more flexible approach to careers within companies – much as the idea of developing consultancy skills is gaining ground). The basic fact remains, however, that some managers make better interims because of their personality and outlook on life.

It is possible, however, to boost your chances by ensuring that you present yourself in the best light to the interim firms that fill assignments.

WHAT QUALITIES DOES AN INTERMEDIARY LOOK FOR?

The starting point for anyone considering a career as an interim manager should be a deep understanding of what the role entails. But, no matter how brilliant, you are unlikely to get a chance to prove yourself unless you can convince the intermediary to give you the opportunity.

Those with experience of recruitment firms know how tough it can be to even get on the shortlist of people presented to the client company. So, the first step is to understand what it is that firms specializing in interim placement are looking for.

'In general they are looking for people who can make things happen', says PA's Stuart Cain. The interim firm is looking for a spectrum of skills to fit different situations, but there are certain common characteristics. According to PA Consulting, the ideal candidate should:

1 Interview well: if they don't grab us at interview, then they probably won't grab the client. They should have good presentation skills and be well presented. They should be enthusiastic and real – you can't bluff in this job.
2 Have a good track record. They must stand out from the crowd in their CV. We want to see they can operate at the right level; that they have a variety of experiences, perhaps some trouble-shooting; basically a project-based CV, one that shows a strong record in change management.

3 Have good interpersonal skills. It's no good being completely abrasive, even if it's a tough job. You have to work with what's there. If it's a 6-month assignment, you really have to get the best from the people: someone who's good at active listening and then putting it together into a plan; someone who can make a rapid assessment of a good way forward and then keep adjusting it week by week.

> *We don't turn away a good finance controller.*

4 Be able to make things happen. It's a hard quality to explain, but after a while you recognize it when you see it. People are either leaders or followers. In some situations we're looking for a good No. 2. We won't turn away a good financial controller, for example.

5 Be persuasive: probably operating at one or two rungs below their level of competency.

6 Look the part, it helps. It's hard to sell someone scruffy as a good corporate manager.

7 Clearly, have keen minds. They are a very bright bunch of highly energetic people. But they also have to know when to shut up. Often, they enjoy being outspoken. Some assignments need someone outspoken more than others in order to do the job.

8 High energy levels are a prerequisite. Time is of the essence. Being charged out on a day-rate makes the IM role very visible. The invoice has to be signed off every week. They are away from home a lot, and work long hours. The success of any project often comes down to the energy levels of the leader. They tend to be thrashing about the country – and they tend to be fairly lean and fit people in the 45 to 55 bracket. It's not an easy option by any means.

WHAT SHOULD YOU EXPECT FROM AN INTERMEDIARY?

Those who use specialist interim firms – whether as interim managers or clients – should expect much the same standards from the person on the other side of the desk.

One point that cannot be emphasized enough, here, is the need to do some research. It is not advisable to use the first interim firm you happen to stumble across. A little digging around can pay dividends. Depending on your level of seniority and area of expertise, some intermediaries will suit you better than others. It is well worth talking to interims on their books and clients who have used their services.

Moreover, you will usually find that certain intermediaries have better contacts in particular industries or disciplines. It is worth finding out, for example, whether they regularly place interims in City firms or are more oriented towards engineering or manufacturing firms.

The following is a checklist of what the individual and the client should expect from an interim intermediary. In particular:

- Are they interim specialists, or do they just dabble in this market?
- How long have they been active in this area? How many assignments have they filled?
- Which part of the market do they cater for? Do they concentrate on director level and just below or do they cover middle management roles as well?
- Are they part of an international network, or simply a national or regional operator?
- Do they have a published code of conduct?
- Do they have a convincing client list and appropriate endorsements from senior managers?

- Are they part of a larger recruitment operation with access to search and selection expertise? Or are they a stand-alone operation? (Either can be effective, depending on what you hope to achieve.)
- Do the people you are dealing with have any experience of interim management themselves? Have they ever carried out an interim assignment to know what is involved?

The intermediary should perform the following tasks:

- Marketing your credentials to potential clients.
- Keeping you regularly updated with progress reports.
- Negotiating your fees.
- Providing you with a full brief of the assignment – including a frank analysis of the 'real conditions' on the ground.
- Providing legal advice and other support when requested.
- Collecting fees – including payment to you regardless of disputes with the client.
- Arbitrating in any dispute.
- Contacting regularly to find out how the assignment is progressing.
- Someone to talk to *in extremis.*
- Identifying the next assignment in advance wherever possible.

In addition, some firms also organize social gatherings such as lunches which provide excellent networking opportunities to meet other interim managers.

CASE STUDY

An interim solution to Impress

Based in London, the Impress Group imports and manufactures picture frames, photographic products and chemicals as well as office machinery for small print houses. Clients include Boots, WH Smith and SupaSnaps.

When the company took over Intercraft early in 1998, it quickly became evident that a programme of rationalization was needed. The Group's operations were spread over several sites within a 25-mile radius, and the company was leasing expensive warehousing for imported goods.

One of the new management's first decisions was to reduce this cost as quickly as possible and make better use of the space. With all the other demands on management after the acquisition, there was no senior member of staff available to implement the required changes.

A campaign to recruit an executive capable of handling this project was ruled out on the basis that it would take too much time and was not necessary for a short-term project. The company chose instead to appoint an interim manager.

Within a week, Mike Howell, a senior executive with experience in engineering, manufacturing and service industries was on board.

'Hands-on' management

Mike Howell, epitomizes the term 'hands-on' management. 'The key to being effective is to have staff on your side within a week of joining the company', he says. 'My first 2 weeks are spent planning, thinking, looking at the site and talking to people.

'As an interim manager, there is the time to listen to everyone – something that the average staff manager does not do. I discuss their problems and ideas and by establishing a rapport can 'sell in' the changes and convince the workforce that any changes will be beneficial even if they involve downsizing.'

As an outsider Howell offered a fresh pair of eyes. He could ask simple questions without embarrassment and when faced with the answer 'because we always have' could probe further. At a previous job he discovered a computer fault which was producing orders for the wrong stock quantities and had been doing so for 2 years.

The first task at Impress was to reorganize the site and decide on appropriate racking. A narrow aisle system was chosen to maximize the space available. Suitable forklift trucks were bought, which could enter the aisles sideways, and staff trained to use them. Health &

Safety procedures were put in place. The amount of work in progress was reduced and production tailored to make the correct batch quantity. Week 3 involved getting quotations, obtaining approvals and placing orders.

Have staff on your side within a week of joining the company.

The movement of goods from the rented warehouse in Coseley to Telford was completed by the end of February, resulting in an immediate saving of £130 000 per annum.

The next stage involved moving 20 members of staff from Tipton to Telford. This has involved talking to the managers and ensuring that their personal requirements are met wherever possible, installing a new computer and telephone system and changing items such as office lighting to be VDU compatible. A minibus service for those staff who do not want to drive to Telford has been organized.

Decisions on the capital outlay, the budget for consumables and projected savings are all part of Howell's job. Although he reports to the financial director, he is essentially his own boss and is given the authority to make all the decisions necessary to complete the project.

'I have worked in many different industries and therefore I do not have to keep re-inventing the wheel', says Howell. I have tried and tested the solutions I recommend elsewhere and have also had to implement them so I know they work.

'Because I am away from home, I work long hours and so my client gets excellent value for money.'

Having almost completed the rationalization of space, Mike is now negotiating with architects, town planners and contractors to build another wing on the factory so that he can close the Coseley site and provide Impress with further savings.

According to Dick Reynolds, Chief Executive at Impress, the group is growing fast and is hot on the acquisition trail. 'With the speed of change in the group, we are bound to find that we lack specific management skills at certain times. Using an interim manager for the change programme has worked well and I am sure we will be using that solution again.'

Interim humour

'Ever employ a sea squirt? The juvenile sea squirt floats through the ocean searching for a suitable rock or coral to cling to and make its home for life. When it finds its spot and takes root, it doesn't much need its brain any more, so it eats most of it. It's sometimes like having tenure in a job.'

NOTES TO CHAPTER 6

1 Donkin, Richard, 'The permanent temp is a Handyman', *Financial Times*, 16 March 1994.
2 Golzen, Godfrey, *Interim Management*, Kogan Page, 1992.
3 Altman, Wilf, 'Servant takes masters role', *The Times*, 24 July 1997.
4 Golzen, Godfrey, *Interim Management*, Kogan Page, 1992.
5 Eadie, Alison, 'Stop-gap executives are all the go', *Daily Telegraph*, 12 March 1998.
6 Watts, Sally, 'Business brains for hire', *The Times*, 9 February 1995.

The assignment

The assignment life cycle

Quick wins and hidden heroes

Preliminaries: intelligence gathering

Phase 1: Getting to know one another

Phase 2: Defining objectives

Phase 3: Setting milestones

Phase 4: Implementation

Phase 5: Exit

An interim has to call the shots and take responsibility. He or she has to be big enough to tell the company if something will not fly and, if it will not listen, must be prepared to walk away. You cannot afford failure as you are only as good as your last job.

JOHN POLLARD, interim manager.[1]

The essence of the interim manager's role is the instant management resource. To justify his day rate, the interim must be able to step in at a moment's notice.

'I like to think of them as being parachuted into alien territory, their skills strapped to their belt, ready to hit the ground running', says Martin Wood of Boyden Interim Executive, of his interims. 'But it is what happens on the ground that really counts.'

THE ASSIGNMENT LIFE CYCLE

Talking to interim managers, most seem to agree that there are a number of distinct stages that are passed through during the course of an assignment. While no two assignments are ever the same (a fact that interim managers seem to revel in), they say there are some common characteristics in the 'life cycle' of an assignment. It starts the moment the interim arrives on site.

Says one experienced interim: 'Being an outsider, you can walk into any part of the business and say, "Who are you? What do you do? Why are you doing that? Why are you doing it that way and not that way?" Now, clearly, if you have been managing director of something for 6 months or 12 months you can't do that, or if you come from another bit of the business it's a bit difficult to do, but coming in as interim it does give you the ability to go back to basics and ask them why they are doing things.

'You will always find areas of the business where they are doing it just because they've always done it, and for no other reason. No one's ever re-engineered it and if you have the experience of working in another sector in other companies you can always import a good idea. Without fail, it works every time. So, you just have to pick on a few of those and get those going

141

and that makes you more credible, it makes management more comfortable that they have found the right person, it just adds credibility to the whole situation and you know, gets you started. If you see a good idea, you don't wait, you just get on with it, you don't write a strategic plan around it, you'd probably write it and plan afterwards.

> *If you see a good idea, you just get on with it.*

'The middle is just like any other job, you know, things work, things don't work, go back to the board, change things, the structures changing. Its actually making the changes, its committing the changes, getting the team on board, strengthening the team, getting it on course, you know, remotivating, redirecting whatever ... and that obviously takes the time. Then you've got the exit.'

Some people will argue that the analogy of a military operation is inappropriate here. However, as a number of recent interventions by the United Nations and other humanitarian operations have shown, the absence of clearly defined targets can all too often lead to a state of drift.

> *Parachute in, secure the defined objectives, and get out.*

The upshot in most cases is that the initiative becomes bogged down and quickly reverts to a state of reacting to events instead of shaping them. Clearly, there is no direct comparison in terms of the human cost involved, but the interim manager, too, can ill afford inertia or drift on an assignment. The name of the game for the effective interim is to parachute in, secure the defined objectives, and get out when the job is done.

Typically, an assignment will go through the following cycle, starting with a preliminary stage prior to accepting or being selected for the position.

Preliminaries: Intelligence gathering

- Assignment briefing.
- Interview with client.
- Administration/contract/fee negotiations, etc.

Phase 1: Getting to know one another

- Induction into company, including background materials and introductions to team and direct reports
- Drafting of business objectives and a preliminary plan of what the assignment will achieve.

Phase 2: Defining the mission

The interim makes an initial assessment of the situation on the ground – it may not be the same as in the brief. This usually takes between 1 and 4 weeks, and includes:

- Audit of staff, the business unit, or department, or the project and a rapid assessment made
- This is then fed back to the board of directors
- Senior management buy-in. It is at this stage that they say 'yes'. If they can't agree there has to be a parting of the ways.

Phase 3: Setting milestones

This is when the real planning begins. With a mandate from senior management (often the chief executive himself) the interim can get on with what needs to be done. In the third phase the interim:

- Prepares a more detailed strategic plan with milestones for the next 6 months.
- Establishes credibility and tries to win the trust of staff.
- Champions are identified inside the management structure and brought on board.

- Identifies, and plans for, obstacles – for example, infrastructure shortcomings, or lack of resources.
- Neutralizes or removes resistance, if necessary.

Phase 4: Engagement

This is the middle part of the assignment. In Phase 4, the interim and the team start work on the implementation of the plan. Typically, it will include:

- Some quick wins. These give the team a sense of achievement and help build morale (often there are opportunities which present themselves in the first couple of days and can be written into the plan later).
- Getting the team on board and motivating them.
- Celebrating successes as each milestone is passed.
- Mentoring direct reports, so that the interim's experience rubs off on younger managers who will carry on the work after the assignment is over.
- Working towards a clear objective – typically a challenging target set by the interim.
- Regular progress reporting to the senior management and the interim intermediary.

Phase 5: Exit

This is the final phase of the assignment. By now, the milestones in the plan will have been achieved, but the interim must ensure that the company does not become dependent on him. Some projects come to a natural end, but with others the interim has to manage his own exit. This phase may include:

- Recruiting a permanent replacement.
- Grooming an internal replacement for the role.
- Setting an end point – maybe a date, an objective, or some other event or development (this should also be the signal for

the intermediary to begin the marketing for the next assignment).

- Evaluating the success of the assignment (often a report to the senior management team).
- Saying goodbye.

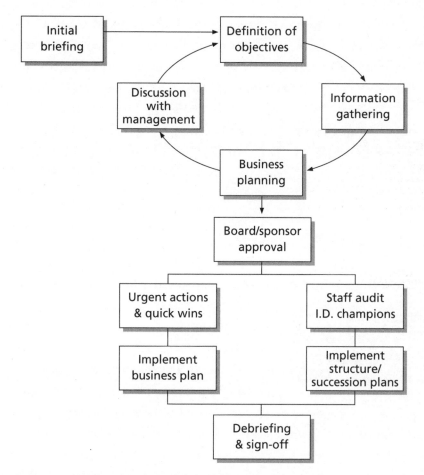

Fig 7.1   Interim assignment process – change project.

QUICK WINS AND HIDDEN HEROES

However, these phases are often overlaid. The most important issue for the newly appointed interim is to establish his credibility and identify people he can work with. Two vital issues will occupy the interim in the first few hours and days, even before he gets down to the task in hand.

'Where are the quick wins? There's always something in the first 2 days – a good idea that no one's listened to, or something that you can action quickly' says PA Consulting's Stuart Cain. 'The advantage of being an outsider is that you can walk onto the shop-floor and ask naïve questions. The MD can't do that. But, the interim manager can ask people why they are doing it that way. You usually find it's because they have always done it that way. Without fail, you can always import one good idea from outside. This builds credibility. You take these opportunities and write them into the plan afterwards.'

'Also, from day 1, the interim manager is looking for champions. So, in parallel with the planning, as soon as you walk in the door, you are starting to assess who are the good guys, who are the bad guys, who can I work with, who's helping me, who's standing in the way, what are the strengths and weaknesses, what are the opportunities that no one's actually latched on to, and quick wins because everyone needs some successes in the first couple of weeks, and there's always something that you can improve.

> From day 1, the interim manager is looking for champions.

'So, if you come from the outside, with the experience of having done projects before, then I guarantee you will see something in the first couple of days that you can improve on fairly easily. It might be cost cutting, or it might be introducing a good idea no one's listened to before.'

Company doctor, David James, calls them 'hidden heroes'. The success of the project and the salvation of the company can often depend on identifying them.

'As I cross the threshold of every new job, I always say to myself "I am looking to find the people in this company who will work with me to sort this out, and I do not exclude anyone",'[2] he says.

'You don't find them by sitting in your own office. You have to get out. The early days of a project are very largely about sitting down in every nook and cranny of the company and saying "talk to me. Tell me what you are doing and why you are doing it" '.

PRELIMINARIES: INTELLIGENCE GATHERING

The preliminary phase of an interim assignment is really one of information gathering. Most of the work at this stage should be done by the interim firm or intermediary (assuming there is one involved).

It is in this early part of the process, before the interim has even been put forward for the assignment, that the intermediary really earns its money. It is in this phase that the initial parameters for the assignment are determined.

Although it typically happens very quickly, often in just a few hours from the initial inquiry, the procedure is an intensive one, involving a period of close consultation with the client company. It will normally result in a fairly detailed brief, including the job description and likely duration of the assignment. Once this has been agreed with the client, the intermediary will match the requirements with its database and draw up a shortlist of candidates.

Shortlisted candidates are then briefed by the intermediary. This includes the industry background and market position of the client company, and the circumstance surrounding the appointment. At this stage, however, the interim has not yet been selected and so confidential or commercially sensitive information will not be provided.

Part of the process involves a judgement about the best sort of approach to the assignment. 'Interims are a bright bunch of energetic people who, if asked, or prompted or given the opportunity will be outspoken, but they've got to know when to shut up and listen because if they are outspoken at the wrong moment then the team walks out says Stuart Cain. Then they aren't going to achieve anything.'

'Now, for some assignments you are going to need people who are more outspoken than for other assignments. They are probably all the same types of people underneath, it's a question of how direct they are going to be.'

The next step involves an introduction – or interview – with the client contact. This will be organized by the intermediary, who will typically facilitate the interview process. The degree of formality surrounding the interview is something that varies according to the culture and preferences of the client. It is usually an area where the intermediary uses his judgement.

Often, the selection process involves more than one interview, and frequently the chief executive or members of the senior management team will be directly involved in the selection decision. (This is very important, as without the support of senior management the interim will be unable to function effectively.)

Once the client is satisfied that a candidate is suitable, terms of engagement are agreed, including fee and time-scales. The assignment then moves speedily on to the next phase.

PHASE 1: GETTING TO KNOW ONE ANOTHER

Now that the interim has been appointed, it is vital that he or she be brought up to speed as quickly as possible. At this stage, the intermediary provides a more detailed brief. One interim management firm, for example, includes the following:

● *The details of the lead contact at the client company* – the person to whom the interim will report. (This is not always the same as the person who made the initial approach.)

It is the job of the intermediary to understand the internal politics. It has to be stated pretty clearly at that stage that, if they really want the interim manager to do a proper job, then he's got to have clear objectives and a clear mandate.

Says one experienced interim 'You have to ask: "what are the politics here and what does the client really want to achieve?" When the going gets tough, as it will, what is this managing director going to do? Who is he going to turn to and say: "right, I have decided I need to fire this person or close that or whatever? Do I have the authority and by the way I need another million pounds", or whatever it is. Is the interim here because the MD doesn't want to do it.

> He's got to have clear objectives, clear mandate.

● *A detailed description of the client organization*, including:
  – precise explanation of where the interim assignment fits into the client organization
  – brief history of the company
  – market position and main competitors
  – location of sites/number of employees
  – financial details
  – corporate structure – including how the client company fits into a larger corporate entity, group or parent company

    – key people in the senior management team

    – recent company press cuttings.

- *Background*: including a brief description of the circumstances in which the appointment has occurred and the current state of the business.
- *Business case*: why an interim solution has been proposed, and what the key objectives of the assignment are, including time-scales, and how the interim appointee is to be introduced to staff.
- *Key contacts*: clearly defining the reporting lines – both up and down.
- *Targets*: what the client expects the interim to achieve in the course of the assignment.

This phase also includes the first few days in the post. The intermediary should ensure that all the arrangements are in place to enable the new appointee to make a smooth landing in the job.

This is all the more important because the time-scales are so tight. On occasions, an interim manager can be in post within 2 or 3 days of hearing about the job. Typically, the interim firm will liaise with the client's human resources or personnel department to ensure that the induction goes smoothly.

Advice on how to handle the first few days is the subject of a number of books. Most interims will have their own way of making an impression in the first few days.

The following observations come from David James, one of Britain's best-known company doctors, and himself no stranger to stepping into an unfamiliar corporate culture. He believes that, since 1984, he has helped secure 23 000 jobs in otherwise insolvent companies and has ensured the repayment of £850 million in bank debt.

In a recent interview, he explained how he dealt with a typical first day. Addressing the workforce at Sears Group's British Shoe Corporation, where he was brought in as executive chairman, a worker observed: 'Mr James, you don't know anything about retailing. How could you possibly come and be our chairman?'

His response, he explained, was to point out that his lack of knowledge simply reinforced his need of assistance from the employees. 'I am not going to step down from here until I hear from you what has gone wrong here', he told them. 'You all know your company is at risk . So, tell me what you think has gone wrong.'

Frankness, according to James, is absolutely essential. Too often, the new appointee is fobbed off with half-truths about what is really going on.

One issue in particular requires careful consideration: should staff be told from the outset that the person coming in is an interim manager?

There are pros and cons on both sides. One advantage of introducing the appointee as an interim is that it avoids confusion over succession issues. In particular, a manager who feels he has been passed over for a promotion is more inclined to stay if he knows the person above him is a temporary appointment. The downside, however, is that the temporary nature of an interim's position may undermine credibility and authority (staff know that he will be gone in 6 months).

For these and other reasons, this issue is handled differently depending on the circumstances. Once again, it is usually an area where the intermediary's judgement is invaluable. In many cases staff are unaware that person is an interim manager. If the individual is clearly good at the job, the people below will tend to accept him. Often, they are pleased to have someone who is prepared to take decisions.

As one interim explains: 'If they have been without clear

leadership for any time, they are just pleased to have someone take charge. People come to you with their questions and a backlog of questions and issues. Within a couple of hours you're into the daily routine. Later on, you can walk the floor and talk to people about what they do.'

But, if the position is politically sensitive, it may be better to tell staff that it's an interim appointment. That way, the assistant sales director, for example, won't get upset because he thinks someone has been brought in over his head. If he's not quite ready for the job, he can learn from the interim and he knows the post is still open.

It comes back to the succession issue. One of the great advantages of interim managers is that they won't upset the succession plan. It can be stated explicitly that the interim will coach people while there. Often, the mentoring role is a stated objective. One recent client specified that this was part of the assignment. We want a project director, they said, but we want him to train our project managers to perform the role in future.

PHASE 2: DEFINING OBJECTIVES

In the second phase of the assignment, the interim manager begins to get down to the nitty-gritty. This is the first real opportunity he has to assess the situation for himself. Until this point, all he has to go on is what he has been told by the client, and the intermediary. In theory, this should be a comprehensive assessment of the situation. However, there are a multitude of factors that can distort this reading of the situation.

They include everything from political manoeuvring within the client company to attempts to camouflage incompetence – even fraud. In phase two, the interim evaluates the situation for himself. Typically, the interim will be carrying out a form of mental audit of the organization from the moment he steps over the threshold – sometimes even before this when he meets the client. During Phase 2, this audit process comes more to the fore. It usually doesn't involve an inventory of what's in the building, but is more a case of taking stock of what's there to work with.

At this stage, too, the interim will be looking to validate the brief he has been given. Sometimes, the conclusion he reaches is not the same as that reached by the client. This is one of the reasons that objectivity and independence are such important qualities for an interim. The interim must use his own professional judgement to assess what, if anything, is wrong and the best way to put it right. Most interims have a nose for bad smells in an organization. It is part of their role to speak out if they see something that is not right. Indeed, it is in their own best interest to do so since it is their job to sort it out – and their professional reputation that's on the line.

Out of this audit process, a plan emerges. At this stage it will not go into a huge amount of detail, but it will set out the challenge and the way the interim intends to tackle it. In many respects this phase is akin to what a consultant would do. It culminates in a series of recommendations to the senior management team.

> *Most interims have a nose for bad smells in an organization.*

Unlike the consultant, however, once the recommendations have been approved, it is the interim's job to implement them. This is the crucial difference between the two roles. The consultant makes recommendations but stops short of putting them into action. The interim manager does both. (Sometimes, the interim will be brought in after a team of consultants have made their recommendations. Under the right circumstances, the two can complement each other very effectively.)

Once the interim has made his assessment of the situation and reported back to the client (usually at board level), the client should sign off on his approach so he can get on with the job. But sometimes the conclusion he reaches is not the same as that reached by the client. This is one of the reasons why objectivity and independence are such important qualities for an interim. The interim must use his own professional judgement to assess what, if anything, is wrong and the best way to put it right.

On at least one occasion, for example, an interim has identified a major obstacle to the success of the assignment as the person he is supposed to be reporting to. In such cases, the interim must use his influence and professionalism to insist that issues are not papered over.

The intermediary can also play a role here in facilitating the emergence of the 'real issues'. This is a point made by several interim firms.

'The rules of engagement have to be agreed. You have to start out with clear objectives; a clear mandate', says PA's Cain. 'The reporting lines have to be set. It's part of the role of the intermediary to ensure that happens. The interim makes a rapid assessment, and usually this takes between 1 and 4 weeks. After that, he drafts out the business objectives and feeds it back to the board of directors. That's when they say, yes. If they can't agree, there has to be a parting of the ways.

> The interim must use his own professional judgement to assess what is wrong.

PHASE 3: SETTING MILESTONES

Once the objectives and approach have been established, the interim manager moves into the next phase of the assignment. This is when the detailed planning is done. The phrase 'detailed planning' can be misleading here. As with all aspects of the interim role, time is always short.

'Ready. Fire. Aim', is a strategy originated by the management writer Tom Peters to describe the increasing time pressures that affect successful product launches. It could have been invented to describe the interim manager's *modus operandi*. He must be in a constant state of 'readiness', able to step into a post at a moment's notice. Able to shoot from the hip as soon as he arrives. Aiming is something he often does retrospectively.

The third phase of the assignment, however, is an opportunity to at least plot out a route from the place where he starts to the intended destination. It is far less about the minutiae of the traditional planning and budgeting process – which is anathema to most interims anyway – and much more about establishing milestones. These enable him and the team that he is fast creating to know they are on track. The milestones also provide victories along the way which can be celebrated and which will help fuse the team into a unit and lift morale.

To some extent, of course, setting the milestones is setting the performance targets by which the interim will be judged – at least within the team or department. (Senior management will be more concerned about whether the overall objectives are met.) It is important that the milestones set represent a balance of 'stretch' or challenge, without being impossible to achieve, otherwise they are missed and result in demoralized staff. A good interim manager will know how to push it without creating an impossible target.

PHASE 4: IMPLEMENTATION

There is surprisingly little to say about the implementation phase. This is the stage where the interim and the team really

> They are goal-oriented, and performance driven.

have to roll up their sleeves and get on with it. Each assignment is so different that it is impossible to do much else but point out some typical features of interim assignments.

These include the following observations:

- During the mission–critical phase of an assignment, most interim managers report working very long hours – usually including weekends and evenings.
- Most are quite happy to relocate for the duration of an assignment (one estimate suggests that 75 per cent of all interim assignments in the US involve temporary relocation).
- Interims tend to be a physically fit and professionally hardy bunch, which enables them to achieve remarkable targets.
- They are goal-oriented, and performance driven.
- They have high energy levels and remarkable endurance – especially those in their late 50s and early 60s.
- They would be bored rigid if they weren't doing something they regard as worthwhile.
- They have good interpersonal skills and lead from the front.
- They are able to motivate others and understand the importance of morale.
- They are decisive, but not divisive.
- They are concerned with practical solutions not theory. If something works in one place, they will use it again somewhere else.
- They pride themselves on getting the job done.
- They freely admit that they have made mistakes, but that they have learned from them.

● They take enormous interest and pride in developing other people.

CASE STUDY

....

Thorn EMI

In the run-up to a proposed demerger involving both a UK and US stockmarket listing, the music group Thorn EMI used interim management to provide additional resource. The demanding timetable of the demerger and the departure on maternity leave of a senior financial executive at Thorn added to an already daunting task. There was insufficient resource in-house to cope with the extra demands and it was decided to establish a new group to work alongside the finance function.

Extra accounting expertise was seconded from the Group's auditors Ernst & Young, but the company also required an experienced, qualified managing accountant. This manager needed to be able to learn quickly and manage the new team, which would have to perform under extreme pressure. In addition, the role demanded experience of group consolidations, a good understanding of IT systems and specific corporate finance experience in the requirements of Super Class 1 circulars and listing particulars.

Such an appointment would not be easy, even with time to play with. No in-house solution was identified and long-term recruitment using executive search was ruled out due to the immediacy of and short-term nature of the assignment. Once the demerger was completed, there would be no on-going position for the executive.

Thorn EMI turned to interim manager Andrew Emmet. His brief was to ensure the objectives of the demerger accounting team were met and that all financial information was prepared within the tight deadlines and budget allocated.

Emmet joined Thorn some 8 months prior to the scheduled demerger, and managed a team of newly qualified accountants together with a consultant accountant. When he took up the appointment, a number of key issues, such as the structure of Thorn and treatment of intercompany debt had not been decided. One of his first tasks was to take up and resolve these issues with the Group's treasury function and make appropriate recommendations to senior management.

As the demerger team had undergone several staffing changes immediately before the critical period of the project, staff training, bringing new recruits up to speed and team building were all central to its success. Careful planning was essential.

In the space of just 5 months, the project effectively involved 5-year-end, interim and quarterly reporting processes. Due largely to the need to restate historical data, too, each of these would have to be revised several times as the process developed. By careful scheduling of work – including extensive liaison with the reporting accountants Ernst & Young, the company's lawyers, Rowe & Maw, and the Group's brokers SBC Warburg – the team managed to condense several weeks' work into one.

After 5 months of intensive activity, Emmet's team had all the required financial information prepared ahead of time for when Thorn EMI announced the details of its demerger. The consolidation ledgers were fully analysed, split and rebuilt for the two new groups – an enormous task, given the size of the Group.

According to Stephen Young, Thorn EMI's Group Financial Controller, Andrew quickly got up to speed and managed the team to its objectives. Overall, the demerger process worked well and Andrew played a key part in that.

Following the announcement of the demerger, Emmet worked on proofing the final documents and finalized the file for handover to both EMI and Thorn executives.

PHASE 5: EXIT

It is in the nature of the interim manager's job that no matter how successful he has been in a post, there comes a time when he must bow out. (If he does not do so, he ceases to be an interim manager and becomes a regular – albeit probably underemployed member of staff.)

In fact, according to the intermediaries, very few interims actually stay on in permanent posts. In reality, of course, this could be misleading, as anyone who stays cannot be classified as an interim. In all probability, there will be some people who start out as interim managers, but then decide that they would prefer to remain with the company. However, despite what some more cynical observers might suggest, this group does seem to be a minority.

It is certainly true that, talking with 'professional interims' – those who have had more than three or four assignments – they have no interest in a permanent position, although they report that they are often asked to stay. It

> *There comes a time when he must bow out.*

is this hard core of professional interims that are the most vociferous about managing the exit. They know that it is part of the professionalism of the interim role to bow out gracefully, and to leave the business in a better state than they found it.

Says one experienced interim: 'You must ensure the company doesn't become dependent on you. Some projects come to an end, but if it's a line management job, you may need to hire someone to take over. This is an important part of the IM's assignment. IM can help in interviewing and shortlisting, which can be a very time-consuming process. Once the change is implemented, you should be looking to make yourself obsolete. Once the targets have been met, it's time to get out and the quicker the better.'

Otherwise, if an interim remains in post too long, his presence can start to upset the balance of the management team. Explains Stuart Cain: 'The interim manager should be too strong an individual for the role; he will have been deliberately chosen because he is overqualified for the job. If he stays too long in the post, he will start to interrupt the succession planning of the organization and its structure. Most interims know when they're getting to the end of an assignment. In fact, the interim will usually trigger his own exit. Or the recruitment drive will have identified the right replacement.'

Either way, making a clean exit is an integral part of the interim manager's role. This is often made easier by a quality possessed by many interims that can best be described as 'professional restlessness'.

The following comments are fairly typical.

'The boring bit about business life is when it's all up and running, and its nice and smooth, and all you are doing is just sort of caretaking, it', says one interim manager. 'I like the challenge of sorting things out, getting in there and making change and that's what you get from interim management. It also gives me a bit of freedom because I do have some other business interests.'

Jokes another: 'I had attention deficit disorder before it was fashionable.'[3]

CASE STUDY

London Electricity's success with first interim manager

Interim management may not roll off the tongue in many UK corporate boardrooms as a solution to a company's dilemma. As a new resource it is only just starting to make its presence felt.

Despite interim management being a relatively unknown resource in the UK, with only 11 per cent of companies aware of its existence, the need for temporary but sharp and timely management has never been greater.

In July 1997, faced with an imminent tough sales target that would influence its long-term presence, London Electricity plc hired its first ever interim manager, Norrie Johnston.

London Electricity's strategy is to become a significant national player in energy supply (gas and electricity) as the industry moves towards full, deregulated competition.

Working to achieve this ambitious aim is LE's Energy Retailing Group, and in the course of the last 9 months they experienced first-hand the value of having their own interim manager to help them achieve their vital spring sales campaign target.

Gill Golding, General Manager of the Energy Retailing Group explains that, for the interim manager she would appoint, it was never going to be an easy sales target.

'The environment in which we operate is highly competitive and unsettled, due largely to the looming full deregulation the industry faces in 1998,' she said. 'The over 100 kW (or business) market has been competitive for 2 years now, and business customers have realized they are free to choose their energy supplier.

'Competition has meant that we have to offer more than just price, and we had to totally re-evaluate the package we offer customers. The market is highly segmented, competition is fierce, with margins slashed to secure long-term business, and a lot of customers are confused by what they are being offered.'

The most important sales campaign for the Energy Retailing Group is the spring sales campaign lasting from November through to April, although planning for this year's campaign began as early as last May. The largest proportion of the year's business is traditionally signed up in this campaign.

Golding herself had been asked to head a long-term strategic project and knew that entrusting the role of campaign manager to just anyone was not an option. It would take a professional interim manager to successfully manage the Group's day-to-day business with a clear grasp on how the target could be met.

'In this instance, interim management was the way forward,' Golding said. 'We needed a manager who was detached from our complex processes, but who could immerse him/herself in them and bring in their fresh approach.'

'Norrie was what we wanted from an interim manager. His background of high-level management positions, in a variety of industries, gave him an authority when coping with the various disciplines he would encounter in this role. The short-term nature of the task and his lack of "cultural baggage" gave him an objectivity and focus which he would not otherwise have had.'

'Expertise, experience and a "hands on" involvement were part of the challenge of reaching the tough target we had set ourselves, and making it all happen.'

Johnston achieved the goal. By managing and motivating a staff of 90, he has co-ordinated and refined the operations and duties of the range of departments that make up the Energy Retailing Group. His team secured over £150m of new business from the spring campaign, a substantial increase over last year's result.

> In this instance, interim management was the way forward.

Norrie Johnston's background

A chemical engineer by trade, Johnston has worked in a variety of traditional engineering businesses as sales manager, sales director, marketing director and managing director. Four years' ago he decided to embark on a life less 'restrained by corporate culture'.

Married with two children, Johnston, 49, sees interim management as a means whereby companies can gain rapid, cost-effective solutions to their problems. Rapid because someone can be brought in at a few week's notice, cost-effective because the rates charged exclude the usual overheads.

Johnston's first entry into high-level 'gap-filling' was a 9-month post within a division of the Midlands-based multinational, IMI. 'It had problems and having terminated the contract of the existing sales director, it wanted someone to plug the gap and solve those problems until a full-time replacement was found,' he said.

The problems, he says, were lack of sales, lack of results, lack of motivation, too many people and no structure in the sales department. This combination needed a rapid resolution by an experienced sales and marketing person with industrial expertise.

> *He is wholly responsible for their implementation.*

Johnston arrived as sales director with full responsibility for a department of 40. He reviewed sales policy and strategy and repositioned the sales team with more accountability and focus and then helped in the handover to the new director.

An interim manager not only develops recommendations and solutions, he is also wholly responsible for their implementation.

Among the essentials required for success in interim management are mobility and flexibility. It can involve working away from home for months at a time and commuting at weekends, until a project is completed.

A life of constant flexibility and mobility both suits and inspires him. 'I like the challenge of continual change. A new infusion of different environments keeps the adrenaline flowing.'

The key to managing all this change for Johnston is 'a good all-round appreciation of what makes people tick'. Other attributes include: patience, the ability to motivate, speed in assessing people's capabilities, and a good understanding of how a company generates cash and profit.

> *A good all-round appreciation of what makes people tick.*

Least important is knowledge of a product or industry. This can be picked up quickly. However, getting results is paramount. 'There's a lot riding on me,' Johnston said. 'I'm very conscious of how much I'm being paid, and my reputation is critical. I'm only as good as my last success story.'

Results: The 1996/7 campaign

Through improved planning, and better preparation, the 1996/7 Energy Retailing Group's annual spring sales campaign kicked off in a confident fashion. Despite a sluggish market, activity picked up in mid-February and competition was fierce. Notable successes included retaining and growing the Safeway account, worth £30 million, which was quickly superseded by LE's largest ever contract, with Thames Water, worth £100m over the next three years. This massive account not only represented a significant step forward for the business, but it helped reinforce other initiatives between the two companies.

The campaign was a success, beating its target and keeping the Energy Retailing Group on track to achieving its 33 per cent growth target for 1996/97.

What LE achieved

- Campaign sales target achieved £330 million – an excellent effort, and making the year's target growth of 33 per cent all the more feasible.
- Negotiated three of the 'big five' targets: Thames Water, Safeway and BR.
- Conducted a noticeably smoother and more professional campaign with a greater emphasis on working to a strategy and focusing on specific areas rather than random, but not always fruitful, opportunities.

NOTES TO CHAPTER 7

1 Eadie, Alison, 'Stop-gap executives are all the go', *Daily Telegraph*, 12 March 1998.

2 Houlder, Vanessa, 'The hunt for hidden heroes', *Financial Times*, 4 February 1998.

3 'More hired guns wear CEO hats', *New York Times*, 28 June 1998.

The future of interim management

8

The future of careers

The interim manager as developer

Tomorrow's interim manager

Developing tomorrow's interim managers

The job-sharing interim

The virtual interim

**There is a new phenomenon
sweeping the global business world:
a serious shortage of qualified
people to meet the fast-growing
needs of corporations.**[1]

MIKE JOHNSON,
Economist Intelligence Unit report

THE FUTURE OF CAREERS

Once upon a time, careers were a relatively simple matter. You learnt a trade and you practised it for your working lifetime, often for a single employer. It's a lot different today. The norm is increasingly frequent changes of employer and a number of significant career shifts. Even people who stay with a single employer for a long period are likely to experience frequent shifts in the nature and content of their work. Many multinational companies routinely shift managers between functions, to make them more rounded, more knowledgeable about the organization as a whole and to bring new thinking into what used to be functional silos.

The reality of management careers in the future is that they will become more and more complex in structure, with frequent, multiple, often confusing choices – indeed, it will often appear that there is no structure. Structure will come from creating options; options will come from gaining flexibility and breadth of experience. In practice, every day brings new career choices in the world of twenty-first century working, because there are always new opportunities to take on additional skills or responsibilities, and to drop others, by delegating them, making them obsolete (for example, by designing systems to replace them) or simply relegating them to a lower level in the hierarchy of importance and urgency. Such choices – we call them career mor-

> *Choices constantly remake the shape of the jobs we do.*

phing – constantly remake the shape of the jobs we do, shape our own and other people's expectation of us and define future possibilities.

In the late 1980s, one of the authors promoted the concept of the manager engaged in a constant search to abandon much of his or her activities, to replace them with new priorities. The figure bandied about at that time was that each manager should be able to dispose of 25 per cent by time of their activities each year, freeing that time for forward-looking, more productive tasks – not least developing others so they can accept greater delegation and maintain the momentum of task disposal. In the coming decade, the evidence we have suggests that 25 per cent is far too little.

Successful, effective managers are likely to end each year with a change of at least a third of their activities over the year before. Pragmatic, results-driven career management, then, will require constant adjustments to the steering wheel. Those managers who fall asleep at the wheel – who take their eyes off the road – may either coast to the side or crash spectacularly.

There is another important skein to this thread, however – the increasing integration of what used to be separate career paths. After graduation, bright men and women typically had to choose between careers as managers or as academics. Research laboratories provided something of a half-way house, but even there, progress usually meant abandoning the knowledge-seeking role for the management stream. (A handful of organizations did provide parallel career streams for researchers and managers, but the concept never became widely accepted.)

The first breaks in this rigid pattern began to emerge with the absorption, by business schools, of senior managers from industry, who wanted to start again down the other track. By and large, this worked well, especially as science parks opened up greater and greater potential for academics to follow the opposite path and set up their own businesses.

In recent years, this integrative trend has begun to accelerate rapidly. Talented people are moving much more freely backwards and forwards between what can be described as knowledge careers and formal management careers. As more employees gather MBAs, NVQs and other formal educational qualifications, the value of knowledge development as an element of managerial progression is raised. Similarly, the knowledge industry has moved beyond universities and business schools into the burgeoning world of consultancy, often with an academic link.

The lubricant between these parallel paths of knowledge careers and formal management careers is often some form of interim career. Figure 8.1 shows all three career paths and some of the more common links between them.

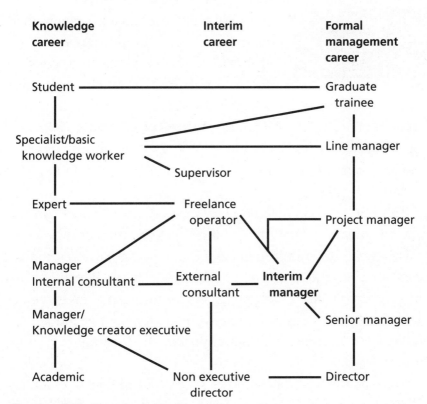

Fig 8.1   The career network

In each of the three paths, there is a gradual acquisition of expertise, status and employment value by the individual. At certain key points in a career, it becomes both appropriate and feasible to switch from one path to another and then, perhaps, back again. Sometimes, the trigger will be an opportunity to gather valuable new experience; sometimes it may be a sudden halt in the current job, for example, through redundancy.

The straight-line career, following one path only, will become increasingly rare. Of course, there will be some people whose natural bent leads them from student to academic without recourse to the 'real' world of business at all, but they will become increasingly uncommon. So, too, will be people who work their way step by step, unremittingly up the management path – for them, the lack of other experience may well be a barrier to the higher levels of management. Interim activities, whether as freelance operator, consultant, interim manager or non-executive director, will be one of the most obvious and practical stepping-stones between the world of knowledge and the world of management.

> *The straight-line career, will become increasingly rare.*

The sequential development of capability and role is illustrated in Figure 8.2.

The implications for people in managing their own careers are considerable. First, they will need to ensure that they view their careers as multidimensional and pay great attention to opportunities for switching tracks in ways that will make them more employable, i.e. that will create increased career value added. Second, they must regard interim activities not as the tail-end of a career but an important and valuable option within it.

The same is true for employers. To build the flexible, multi-skilled expert workforces they will need, companies will need

The role	The task
Student	Acquiring knowledge
Specialist, basic knowledge worker	Using knowledge
Expert	Assimilating/integrating knowledge
Consultant	Sharing knowledge
Knowledge creator	Making knowledge
Academic	Testing knowledge
Graduate	Managing self
Supervisor	Managing outputs
Project manager	Managing complexity
Senior manager	Managing the business
Director	Managing the environment
Non-executive director	Test the management process
Freelance	Offers skill
External consultant	Offers knowledge
Interim manager	Offers experience, track record
Non-executive director	Offers wisdom, challenge

Fig 8.2   A capability chart

to encourage people to switch between career paths as part of their planned career progression. The company will benefit from establishing special relationships with external organizations, such as business schools and consultancies, with which they can maintain a constant interchange of talent. Interim management will then become an opportunity to:

- import skills via people who have never worked there before
- reintroduce into the management structures people who have stepped into a knowledge career path for a period

- place managers, who have limited experience with one company, into temporary positions with another, where they can absorb a whole new range of skills, before returning to their original employer (a form of secondment).

In short, interim management will simply become a routine element in career pathing, for both individuals and the companies that employ them. Looking ahead, it is possible to see a range of new roles and applications for interim managers.

THE INTERIM MANAGER AS DEVELOPER

We have already discussed in some detail the situation where the interim manager is brought in to give a less experienced insider the space to grow into the job. This can be a fairly passive role – simply doing what needs to be done, allowing the less experienced person to make and learn from their own mistakes. More typically, however, the interim will be expected to play a more active role in passing on knowledge, experience and skills to a designated successor.

> *Interim management will become routine in career pathing.*

This can be a very sensitive role. The permanent employee can very easily feel patronized and resentful. To fulfil this side of the task, the interim needs to pay close attention to the following:

- agreeing the purpose and groundrules for a 'learning alliance'
- understanding the diversity of styles that can be adopted in helping someone else grow
- ensuring that the learner takes ownership of the development process.

Agreeing purpose and guidelines

The key here is to define the nature of the transition, that the permanent employee needs to make. This will not always be obvious to them. The transition will often be a mixture of knowledge, experience, thinking patterns, skills and behaviour – sometimes all five. Even if the interim manager were the perfect role model in all these areas, it would probably be less than tactful to suggest so.

Rather, it is better to use the interim's greater experience to help the other person build and act upon a personal development plan that draws on a range of learning resources, including opportunities to try new tasks, a variety of role models both within and outside the company, and more traditional, formal learning, such as business school courses. The interim can also help the employee build a more extensive network of people, upon whom to call, when the interim has moved on.

Styles of helping

The range of styles the interim can adopt is quite wide – there are at least 16. The interim does not have to be adept in all of them, or even to recognize what they are. But they do need to respond appropriately to the learner's needs in terms of: when to be directive (telling or advising) and when to help the learner work it out.

- when to do things on the learner's behalf (for example, make influential connections for them) and when to pass the baton back to them
- when to challenge and when to empathize

As a result, the role will change constantly. Sometimes the need will be for a confidant or sounding board; at other times a shoulder to cry on; at yet others times, someone to goad the learner on to setting and achieving higher personal goals. It all goes to make the role of interim manager/mentor complex, exhilarating and rewarding. The rewards come partly from the satisfaction of seeing someone mature into the position, for which they are being groomed, but equally from the learning that the mentor makes in helping them do so.

Putting the learner in charge

From what has already been said, it should be clear that the mentoring relationship can only succeed if it has the willing commitment of the learner. But, the interim should beware of creating a situation, where the permanent employee becomes too dependent – as can all too easily happen, especially where the learner is much younger and perhaps lacking in self-confidence.

Effective mentors recognize when not to pick up the pieces, when to allow the learner to make their own mistakes. They also establish early on in the relationship the time-scale for their withdrawal and the manner, in which it will happen. If the learner does not seem to be taking charge of the learning process after a reasonable time, then the mentor brings the issue into the open and helps them to think through how they can do so.

> The mentoring role is becoming increasingly common.

One way or another, the mentoring or quasi-mentoring role is becoming increasingly common as a stated or unstated element in the interim manager's role. It is a natural function, which should, we believe, be written in as an expectation within the job description.

TOMORROW'S INTERIM MANAGER

Bill Thompson took a first degree in French. As is so often the case, his initial career made little use of it, except for a short spell as a travel courier – a job he stuck out for the skiing season then decided really wasn't for him. Between university and the travel job, he did a variety of temporary jobs, deliberately learning about different types of work and different companies, for about a year. Nine further months of temping gave him a planned range of experiences in tele-selling and computer trouble-shooting, which led to an offer of permanent employment with the UK subsidiary of a North American telecommunications company.

The company put him on a graduate entry scheme, which provided the rudiments of leadership and management skills. By the time he left, 3 years later, he was a team leader, working on one part of a major software development project. The trigger for his move was an offer to join an IT consultancy, which offered higher pay and a chance to gain wider experience. Bill also felt that the supervisory parts of his job were among the least interesting.

While at the consultancy, Bill took the opportunity to start a part-time MBA. His dissertation was based around the work he was doing, in change management in IT. Consultancy also gave him his first experience similar to interim management – he found himself loaned for 6 months to an engineering company to work alongside a change team. For that period, the engineering company became his home base. While his role was supposed to be expert adviser and an internal manager was supposed to lead the change team, this wasn't the way it worked out in practice. The internal manager spent most of the time with senior managers, smoothing the path of the project, leaving a leadership vacuum, which Bill soon found himself filling. Now more mature, he enjoyed the team leadership role much more than he had expected, and comments from other managers in the company made him feel he had an aptitude for it.

Back in the consultancy, Bill was headhunted again to join a small start-up venture in an area of technology he was unfamiliar with, but where software development was an important support element. It was not a happy move. His ambitions of making a rapid fortune looked increasingly less realistic and he was concerned that the managing director had little real sense of the urgency needed to keep ahead of international competitors, who were working on similar projects.

Bill bailed out of the entrepreneurial venture after less than a year. Some 18 months later, it folded. Bill spent most of this time as an independent consultant and took on a 2-day a week post at a university, working on a research project subcontracted to the university by his first IT employer. When the project reached the stage where new products would be developed within the company, Bill was asked to move across, as interim manager. The deal was straightforward – get the products to the point where they can be marketed, then we'll talk about whether you should stay on as the product manager. In the event, Bill (now in his late 40s) decided he didn't want to become a permanent employee again. He remained in post long enough to develop a successor, then returned to his freelance activities.

By now, Bill had an interim track record. He continued to work as a consultant, taking on a number of short-term interim manager posts, usually part-time, so he could keep both activities going. He also retained links with academia. Then he was offered a full-time interim job as managing director of a newly acquired French subsidiary of a Dutch multinational. Finally, he was making use of his degree subject again!

The French job became permanent and lasted for 4 years, until Bill took early retirement. He had already acquired two non-executive posts, from UK companies with a need to expand in the French markets, and he rapidly added two more on his return to the UK.

Looking forward to the rest of his working career, Bill is able to identify a host of options. Along the way to this point, however, he has learned the value of maintaining a balance between learning and doing, and of planning ahead to create options. He recognizes some poor choices – not least the entrepreneurial venture – but recognizes that even there he has acquired some valuable experience. Several of his employers, both as interim and consultant, have commented that experience of such failure has made him determined never to repeat the same mistakes. Indeed, it is his experience of both success and failure, and the ability to analyse both, which makes his judgement about business so useful.

One lesson he reflects on that he has learned reasonably well is to use the flexibility, which comes from taking greater charge of your own career path, to ensure a healthy balance between work and the other critical lifestreams – social/domestic, personal health, and general development of the mind. It was a message he had taken on intellectually with his first IT company, when a visiting lecturer helped the graduates think about how they would manage their careers. It had only sunk in emotionally, however, when his young son was seriously ill and he had a chance to put his life into perspective. From then on, Bill has undertaken an annual personal review of all his lifestreams, often with the help of a personal mentor – a trusted professional friend who will ask the unaskable. The mentor, perhaps not surprisingly, has had an equally diverse career, but in quite different areas. His career map shows frequent movement between the roles of managing tasks and managing development.

Another lesson has been the power of networks. Almost every career move he has made and all the most interesting jobs he has done, have come about through knowing someone or being known. Again, this was a skill he learned early and has continued to hone since. He expends at least 3 hours a week keeping in touch with old contacts and creating new ones. The Internet has made this much easier, but he knows that the old-fashioned one-to-one meetings, especially over lunch, are still vital.

Bill knows that, historically, most people worked in a 'straight line' career, but he can't understand how they stuck it. Perhaps it was less that they had no choice, he muses, than that they never gave themselves permission to behave differently?

> Another lesson has been the power of networks.

DEVELOPING TOMORROW'S INTERIM MANAGERS

One of many lessons from the experience captured in this book is that an interim career is not for everyone. If you value security, an ordered and disciplined life, have an inbred discomfort at the idea of adventure, then it will almost certainly not be for you.

Yet for an increasing proportion of managers, interim management is going to be a significant part of their future. So how can these people prepare themselves for such a demanding role? Here are some starting points for thinking about the issue:

- Plan your career development to open out a wide choice of employment styles – full-time, part-time, multiple part-time; management, internal consultancy, external consultancy.
- Take opportunities to try different styles of working with each job you have. Inside a company, for example, you typically have an opportunity to participate not just in the traditional (stable) team, but also in project teams, evolutionary teams (long-term project teams where new skills are needed

at each stage of development), virtual teams and development alliances (teams, sometimes only of two people, formed specifically to promote learning).

- Be more proactive in managing the typical career cycle shown in Figure 8.3.

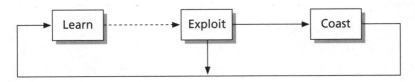

Fig 8.3   The career cycle

People spend very different times at each stage, often inappropriately in the light of their career goals. A good example of coasting is the retired executive, who finds a few non-executive posts, and regards them as a sinecure. Or, the senior manager who becomes a headhunter and milks his or her networks without actively continuing to grow them. If you want to gain the kind of track record that makes you attractive as an interim, you will need to minimize the amount of coasting time and find the right balance between learning and exploiting. The same is true for, say, management consulting. It is quite common for someone to gain some marketable experience and to focus so hard on exploiting it as a consultant that they only realize too late that the sell-by date has passed. Effective interims and effective consultants are constantly topping up their expertise rather than living off it.

One of the phenomena in consulting in the past few years has been the rise of a variety of sources of training and development in consultancy skills. We firmly expect to see similar developments in interim management. 'Interim finishing schools' would help newly appointed interim managers learn how best to carry out the role, including how to manage the entry and exit.

There is an argument, too, to say that companies should also be investing in helping their employees develop interim skills. As universities, TECs, government departments and many private sector enterprises depend more and more on short-term contracts, the issue of the psychological contract becomes less and less easy to ignore. If you take away security of tenure, what do you offer people in return, to secure their loyalty and commitment? The answer seems to be, you offer them employability.

Employability has a number of components, but the two most important ones are *expertise relevant to the external market* and *opportunity scope.* Opportunity scope is the flexibility to use expertise in a variety of circumstances or employment markets. In designing jobs, even at the lowest levels, organizations can, and should, give more consideration to the learning that people can acquire within jobs. Instead of hiring people who are prequalified or overqualified, companies should instead employ people for whom the job will require a stretch. A recent internal study by Microsoft found that the key to high performance lay in constantly stretching people beyond what they thought they could achieve. As soon as someone begins to feel they have mastered a task, the canny leader gives them another task that stretches them yet again.

> Companies should help their employees develop interim skills.

It is possible to do much more, however. A handful of companies now provide people at all levels with an opportunity to learn personal career management skills. Such courses help them to set realistic career goals, to develop flexibility and an understanding of how to select between different options (not just the big changes, like a new job, but the multitude of small choices of which tasks and skills to gain experience of in the current job), and to build their networking skills. Again, this is not simply a philanthropic gesture; it has solid business benefits, not least that encouraging people to take greater charge of their own careers reduces the burden on the human resources function. It also helps the company ease people out, when the fit between the company's needs and what the employee can offer diminishes – the more confidence the employee has and the more sense of career direction, the easier it will be to counsel them out, rather than fire them. If nothing else, this has profound implications for the company's reputation management. How many of your former employees have nice things to say about your company?

Now that interim management is becoming better known and accepted, it makes sense for companies to include in their training for career self-management at least some element of discussion about the interim option. Given that interim employment of some kind is likely to feature in the lives of a high proportion of the organization's employees at some time in their lives, it is pragmatic to help them understand the implications of this kind of working and perhaps even to plan it into their career portfolio. Too many companies avoid these issues, however, in the mistaken assumption that discussing alternative careers outside the organization will stimulate people to leave. If anything, the evidence suggests the contrary – people who have firm career plans are more likely to stick out a period with the company, because they know what they need to learn. The key for the company is to make these ambitions overt and work with the employee to fulfil them within the organization for as long as it suits both parties.

THE JOB-SHARING INTERIM

Finding an interim manager, who has all the experience and competencies a company needs for a particular role can often be difficult. Supposing, for example, you want an engineering manager with specialist experience in lubricants, and fluent Mandarin Chinese, and a good track record in start-up ventures. Rather than give up on any of these criteria, you may find it better to create a job share, in which a senior engineering manager with start-up experience is paired with a Mandarin-speaking lubricant specialist. It needn't cost two salaries – the job is simply split between them as two part-time positions.

> *Job-sharing interims can also be appropriate.*

The key to making this work is the clarity of roles between the two part-time interims (what can be done equally by either and where one partner takes the lead responsibility). One of the benefits is that, when a full-time, permanent manager is appointed, only one of the job-sharing interims may be needed to parallel the manager during the hand-over stage.

Job-sharing interims can also be appropriate when the position involves responsibility for more than one site, especially if those sites are in two or more countries. An interesting option is to have one interim travelling, while the other provides some stability back at the home base.

All of this has been made much easier in recent years by the new digital technologies. One variant of the job-sharing interim is the virtual interim.

THE VIRTUAL INTERIM

The rapid spread of the Worldwide Web makes it possible to use interim managers from much wider afield. Most executives nowadays are used to keeping in contact with operations via their laptop and the Internet, no matter where they are in the world. Many also take advantage of the opportunity to work at home, to ensure they have quiet space to get things done. The reality in most organizations is that managers are less and less visible.

Business management increasingly requires two core skills – the ability to make things happen, through people ('hands on' management) and knowledge management. One form of job share is to divide the interim role along this fault line, with each partner specializing in his or her strongest area, but able to deputize for the other as needed. The knowledge working partner in the job-share is then able to operate, in large part, away from the home base, keeping in constant touch via the Internet.

Typically, the company hires an interim manager for what he knows and what he can do. The virtual interim comes with the added bonus of who they know. He or she is able to refer problems and queries to a group of virtual colleagues, all of whom have different expertise and know-how. So, in buying a virtual interim, the company acquires a network of varied expertise.

Among ways in which the virtual interim might work are:

- in Human Resources, stimulating executives throughout the organization with regular reminders and challenges about their own development, while the company is going through some particularly difficult changes that would otherwise cause them to relegate personal development to the back-burner.
- co-ordinating the efforts of people from different companies, who are working on the same project or joint venture. Being remote can be an advantage here, because it allows the manager to take an objective view. International joint development projects, in particular, often benefit from being man-

aged by a third party who has no history or baggage of working with any of the participating organizations.

● managing the virtual company – although there are very few genuine virtual companies to date, the numbers are increasing rapidly. Virtual companies have very little or no headquarters real estate; they have almost no employees; and they do most of their business on the Internet.

Clutterbuck Associates is an example. It tackles major research and writing projects by creating specialist teams from a network of freelance journalists and academics around the world. It has a presence on several continents, but no offices and no salaries. Project management shifts from continent to continent according to who takes that role at each stage of a contract. It's haphazard, sometimes chaotic, but remarkably effective!

> *The ultimate interim manager belongs to the next electronic era.*

The virtual interim manager is someone who can join the network to take charge of a particular project or group of projects, and may be part-time or full-time (who can check, as long as the work is done?)

The virtual interim will undoubtedly become a more common feature of business as businesses themselves progressively disaggregate into smaller operations and networks. It is inevitable that companies, which rely more and more on remote workers to make products or deliver services, will begin to accept that managers don't need to be on the premises either.

The ultimate of the interim manager belongs to the next electronic era, when artificial intelligence will have progressed to the point that computers can learn to think like their owners – indeed, to assess problems, draw the same conclusions, and suggest the same solutions, as the manager would himself. This is by no means the stuff of science fiction; primitive technologies already exist for this kind of knowledge capture.

Super-managers (the most knowledgeable, most successful, most inspirational or whatever) will effectively be able to clone their minds and their experience, to let the computer make decisions for them. So, one interim manager could conceivably work for several different companies in different countries at the same time. If you can pay, you can have the top guy in the field on your payroll. If the thought appalls, take comfort that it probably isn't going to happen this decade.

NOTES TO CHAPTER 8

1   Johnson, Mike, 'Building and retaining global talent: towards 2002', EIU in cooperation with Hewitt Associates LLC, 1998.

Appendix

Interim managers: a breed apart?

What does it take to be a good interim manager?

Until now there has been no serious investigation into the kind of person that has the personality to make it as an interim manager. The experience of professionals who operate in this area suggest that effective interims are those who enjoy getting results in a short time space, are assertive and not interested in playing politics, are thick-skinned, focused on the job in hand, and able to take initiative. But to date there has been no statistical data which would, for example assist companies with the identification of people who are going to be effective in these often critically important roles.

Recently PA Consulting, the UK provider of interim management services to industry, has decided to take things further by having 96 experienced interim managers complete a work-based personality questionnaire – the PA Preference Inventory (PAPI). PAPI is widely used by PA's global clients for recruitment, management development and team building purposes. The interim managers were compared with a general managerial and professional sample comprising 311 regular managers across a wide range of UK sectors and industries.

One of the first and most striking things which emerged from this research was the degree to which interim managers showed a very distinct typical personality type. While every individual manager has a different make up, taken as a group interim managers were both significantly different in many ways from managers in general, and also fairly homogeneous and similar to one another.

The PAPI measures 20 dimensions of personality and work behaviour, and of these 14 showed highly statistically significant differences between the groups. The major differences are shown in the charts below.

In Fig. A.1 we see that interims emerge as a significantly more autonomous, risk taking and power hungry group than other managers. They appear to have a basic need to control and influence other people. In fact they are at the 81st percentile on this dimension, meaning that the typical interim manager scores more highly than over 81% of other UK managers. One might reasonably guess that this attracts them to short-term assignments, where they are provided with the levers to power in order to make an impact. Equally they tend to see themselves as more competent and confident in a leadership position than the average manager sees himself/herself (78th percentile). They strongly prefer to work in the absence of externally imposed rules and structure, either simply ignoring the rules or making up their own (21st percentile, meaning that nearly 80% of other managers score more highly on need for rules). And they like to make fast decisions (64th percentile), albeit with some calculated risks.

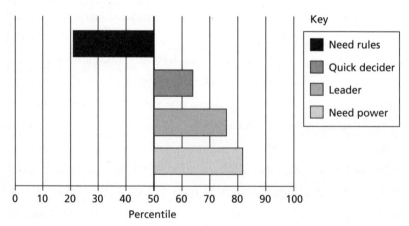

Fig A.1

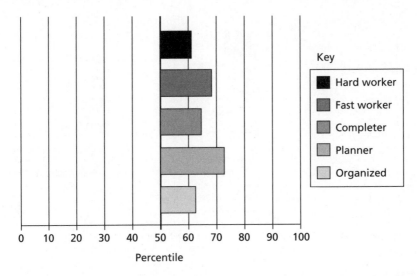

Fig A.2

In Fig. A.2, we see that interim managers strongly value planning – clearly important to the delivery of quick results – with a Completer streak – a personal desire to see things through to fruition. They also describe themselves as more organized types – tidy, able to find files at a moment's notice. In terms of work ethic they see themselves as more dedicated, both in terms of hours and commitment, but also in terms of sheer speed of throughput compared with the typical manager.

In Fig. A.3 we see that interims like change (76th percentile) – no surprise here given their chosen profession. Also they tend to be assertive and ready to confront people and situations, presumably on the basis that is better to speak out – and if necessary ultimately walk away from an assignment – than be associated with a failed initiative.

But perhaps more surprisingly, compared to the typical manager, interim managers appear to be more conceptual/theoretical/creative as opposed to being 'here and now' pragmatic (74th percentile). This in fact was one of the largest differences between the two groups. A possible explanation is in terms of the ability to conceptualize and

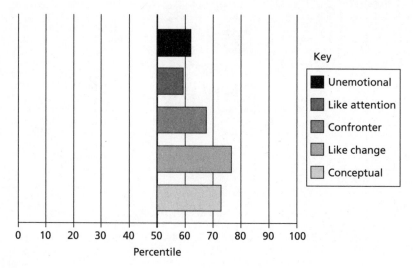

Fig A.3

analyse what may be quite new situations and challenges, and make a clear and thoughtful appraisal.

Another surprising finding (though not such a pronounced difference) was that interim managers like to be noticed and have attention focused upon them. Again with hindsight this may make sense given that interim managers will often be entering very visible, albeit short-term roles, where a lot of attention will be centred. A further surprise was in the area of emotions, where to some extent one would expect an interim to show what he/she was feeling (joy, anger, disappointment) in order quickly to make an impact and progress situations. The reverse was found to be true, with interim managers tending to be more emotionally restrained than 62 per cent of other managers. Perhaps the exhibition of emotion tends to be unproductive in the short-term intensive assignments within which they operate.

In a final six areas interim managers did *not* show any significant differences from managers in general. So they appear to be more (or less) achievement oriented and equally loyal to their boss and organization. Their attention to fine detail is about the same as for the typical manager. Also in terms of social factors (being outgoing, team oriented and close to colleagues) they are typical of managers in general.

In conclusion this research would appear to provide a more informed basis for future identification of interim manager potential, though further investigation is desirable to substantiate some of these initial findings. The PA research program is in fact ongoing, with the next stage a more detailed investigation into those personality characteristics which appear to differentiate really excellent and effective interim managers from the rest. But at least some criteria are emerging which may, if sensibly interpreted and applied, reduce some of the risks associated with selection of interim managers.

Further reading

....

The ATIES Official Guide to Interim Management (1993, 1996) Association of Temporary and Interim Executives (ATIES).

Barret, H. (1995) *The Directory of Interim Management: A flexible, practical and cost-effective resourcing option*. Russam GMS, Executive Grapevine 1997, 1998.

Golzen, G. (1992) *Interim Management – A new dimension in corporate performance*. Kogan Page.

Handy, C. (1989) *The Age of Unreason*. Century Business Books, London.

Henningesen, C. A. and Thompson, J. A. (1995) *The Portable Executive: Building your own job security from corporate dependency to self-direction*. Simon and Schuster.

Interim Management: The GMS market research report (1997) Russam GMS.

Russell, D. (1998) *Interim Management*. Butterworth-Heinemann.

Index

academics 170–2
acceleration, competitive 57–9
accountability 64, 86
acquisitions and mergers 39
Adia 118
advice 63
agility, organizational 4–5, 57
Albemarle 119
Amelio, Gil 15
annual personal review 179
appearance 134
Apple Computers 15, 42
appointment process 125–6, 149–50
arbitration 130
Argos 20
assessment of the situation 143,
    152–4
assignment 139–65
    case study 160–4
    defining objectives 143, 152–4
    exit 144–5, 158–60
    getting to know one another 143,
        149–52
    implementation 144, 156–8
    life cycle 141–5
    matching interim manager to 125–6,
        147–8
    preliminaries 143, 147–8
    quick wins and hidden heroes
        147–8
    range of assignments 29–30
    setting milestones 143–4, 155
Association of Temporary & Interim
    Executive Services (ATIES) 14, 33,
    34, 35, 43
attention 192
attributes of interim managers 89–114

background and personal
    circumstances 73, 92, 99
case study 110–13
changing nature of careers 107–10
interim mindset 104–7
interims vs executive temps 95–7
leadership 100–1
maturity 102–4
money and job satisfaction 101–2
personal qualities 97–9, 189–93
presenting oneself to an
    intermediary 131–2
qualities sought by intermediaries
    132–4
skills most in demand 93–5
authority 65
automation of the British Library
    110–13
awareness, raising 54

Baby Boomers 107–8
balance, healthy 110, 179
Barton Interim Management 119
Birky Plastics 45–6
'booster rocket' role 31–3
Boyden Interim Executive 119, 120–1
Brainforce 118
briefing 126, 148–9, 149–50
Britannia Life 55
British Airports Authority (BAA)
    35–7
British Library 110–13
British Shoe Corporation 151
British Steel 20
buoyant market 77
Burdon, Peter 55
Burrows, Sid 80

business case for interim management 55–7

Cain, Stuart
  chemistry matching 126
  City of London 31
  company doctors 42, 69
  defining objectives 154
  developing people 44–5
  exit 159–60
  internal politics 149, 152
  money and job satisfaction 101–2
  outspokenness 148
  qualities sought by intermediaries 132–3
  quick wins and hidden heroes 147
  'second guessing' 129–30
capability, role and 172–3
career breaks 34–5
career cycle 181
career management 169–70, 172, 181–3
careers
  changing attitudes 107–8
  future of 169–74
  new career rules 109–10
  portfolio careers 76–7, 104–7
  see also employment
Carters Gold Medal Soft Drinks 68
change 191, 192
change management 39–40, 80
chief executives 46–7
choices, career 169
City of London 31
close-downs 40
Clutterbuck Associates 186
coasting 181
Coles, Margaret 14, 73
companies see
  organizations/companies
company doctors 33, 41–4, 68–9, 103
'Company Man' 107
competitive acceleration 57–9
completion 191
conceptual skills 191–2

confrontation 191, 192
Conger, Jay A. 107–8
consultancy 85
  comparison with interim management 46–7, 52–4, 58–9, 62–5, 86, 153–4
  motivation for 76–7
contingency planning 129–30
contingent workers 21–2, 24
contracting 21–2, 23, 74–5
core activities 66
core staff 21, 23
'corporate activity' 59
corporate recovery 33, 41–4, 68–9, 103
costs
  interim managers 86
  permanent staff 59–60, 61
Cox, Tony 82
credibility 125
Cruddace, Gareth 83, 84

Dalton, Archie 104
Davies, David 96
decision-making 190
demerger 157–8
desperation for work 85
development
  of people (mentoring) 33, 44–6, 86, 174–6
  of tomorrow's interim managers 180–3
downsizing 6–7, 7–8, 73, 76, 105
Dunckley, Peter 78–9

Eadie, Alison 53, 55
Emmet, Andrew 157–8
emotion 192
employability 182
employment
  changing nature of jobs 6–7, 21–4, 107–10
  styles 180
  see also careers

Empty Raincoat 5
energy levels 134
Erasmus Graduate School of Business 79
Europe 19, 20–1, 118
evolution of interim management 20–2
Executive Interim Management (EIM) 97–9, 118, 120, 121
executive search 34
executive temps 74–6, 95–7
Executives on Assignment (EoA) 68–9, 85
exit 144–5, 158–60
experience 46–7, 64–5, 86–7, 96, 102–4
expertise relevant to the external market 182
exploiting 181

family businesses 30–1
Farrell, Charlie 43–4
fees
    intermediaries' percentage 123
    money and job satisfaction 101–2
    negotiation of 126–7
    security of payment 127–8
fixed contracts 21–2, 23, 74–5
flexibility 163
    flexing not temping 74–6
    learning to flex 6–7
    role of interim manager 30–1
flexible labour force 21–2, 23
flexible resourcing 52–5
Foot, Richard 64, 65, 82, 93
formal management careers 170–2
frankness 151
free agents 9
full-time positions 77, 85, 159
functional specialisms 94–5
future of interim management 167–87
    developing tomorrow's interims 180–3
    future of careers 169–74
    interim manager as developer 174–6
    job-sharing 184
    tomorrow's interim managers 177–80
    virtual interim manager 184–7

gap management 33, 33–7
Gaskill, Colin 46–7
Generation Xers 107–8, 109
getting to know one another 143, 149–52
Gibsons Greetings Inc. 19, 42
Gilchrist, Keith 46, 63–4
global outlook 5–6
GMS 30, 94, 99
'golden parachuters' 92
Golding, Gill 161–2
Golzen, Godfrey 92, 97–9
Great Universal Stores (GUS) 20
Greythorn Report 54

'hands-on' management 137–8
Handy, Charles 4–5, 22–3, 73, 103
helping, styles of 175–6
Heyden, Karl von der 16
hidden costs 59–60
'hidden heroes' 147–8
Hird, John 34, 52–3, 53–4
Hirst, John 20
Howell, Mike 136–8
human resources 185

IMCOR 44, 77, 121–2
IMI 162–3
implementation 63, 95
    phase of the assignment 144, 156–8
importing knowledge 5–6
Impress Group 135–7
indemnity insurance, professional 129
independence 91, 152–4
induction 128, 143, 150
information technology (IT)
    automating the British Library 110–13

Information technology (IT) *continued*
  BAA 35–7
  outsourcing decisions 66–7
insourcing 7–9
insurance, indemnity 129
integration of career paths 170–2
intelligence gathering 143, 147–8
interim management 11–25
  defining 14–15
  evolution of 20–3
  myths about interim managers
    85–7
  rise of 15–20
  strategic resource 23–4
  use of 23–4, 51, 87
interim mindset 104–7
interim process 121–2
intermediaries 21, 24, 115–37
  choosing and marketing oneself to
    131–2
  expectations of 134–6
  interim process 121–2
  qualities sought by 132–4
  reasons for using 123–31
  role in the assignment life cycle
    147–50
  specialist firms 117–22
interpersonal skills 85, 133
interviews 126, 132, 148

James, David 42, 147, 150–2
James, Kim 81
job satisfaction 101–2
job-sharing 184
Jobs, Steve 15, 42
jobs *see* careers; employment
Johnston, Norrie 161–4
  background 162–3
joint ventures 185–6

Kanter, Rosabeth Moss 5–6
keen minds 134
Kellaway, Lucy 91
Kirkham, Donald 20

knowledge, importing 5–6
knowledge careers 170–2

Lacity, Mary 66–7
Lake, Kevin 36–7
LBO (leveraged buy-out) firms 39
lead contact 149
leadership 100–1, 190
learning 109, 181
  interim manager's mentoring role
    33, 44–6, 86, 174–6
legal advice 128–9
life cycle, assignment 141–5
lifestyle seekers 92
lifetime employment 107–8
London, City of 31
London Electricity 160–4
  background 164
  1996/7 sales campaign 163–4

Mahoney, John 112
management consultancy see
    consultancy
market
  buoyant 77
  expertise relevant to 182
marketing 124–5
Mason, Eric 111–13
matching to assignments 125–6,
    147–49
maturity 102–4
  see also experience
MBA graduates 122
McGregor, Ian 19–20
McKeown, Richard 117
McKinnon, Ian 46
Measures, Mike 81–2
mentoring role 33, 44–6, 86, 174–7
mergers and acquisitions 39
Microsoft 182
milestones, setting 143–4, 155
Millenium problem 127
mindset, interim 104–7
mistakes 103–4

MIT Sloan 19
mobility 163
money see fees
MORI survey 46, 54, 63, 94
motivation of interim managers
    71–87, 99
    flexing not temping 74–6
    free agents 9
    new professionals 79–82
    portfolio people 76–7
    ten myths about interim managers
        85–7
Murray, John 24, 91, 108
    leadership 100–1
    reasons for using interims 57–8,
        58–9
    specialist intermediaries 117–18,
        123
    staffing costs 61, 62
myths about interim managers 85–7

National Coal Board 20
National Lottery Charities Board 40
NBS Interim Management 119
Netherlands 19, 20–1
networking 179
    opportunities 130–1
new professionals 79–82
NHS 82–4
Norwich Union 41

objectives, defining 143, 152–4
objectivity 39, 152–4
O'Conner, Patrick 122
opportunity scope 182
organization 191
organizations/companies
    agility 4–5, 57
    developing interim managers
        182–3
    and future of careers 173–4
    importing knowledge 5–6
    insourcing 7–9
    learning to flex 6–7

organizations/companies *continued*
    reasons for using interims *see* reasons
        for using interim managers
    small and medium-sized 30–1
    virtual companies 186
outsourcing 38, 65–7
outspokenness 134, 148
overqualification 74
ownership 64

PA Consulting Group 24, 31, 75, 93,
    120, 132
    networking opportunities 130
PA Preference Inventory (PAPI)
    189–93
PA Recruitment 119
Pascale, Richard 4, 5
payment, security of 127–8
P-E Incubon 119
Pemberton, Carole 14
people, developing 33, 44–6, 86, 174–6
PepsiCo Inc. 16
permanent managers
    hidden costs 59–60
    interim managers vs 60–2
permanent positions 77, 85, 159
personal career management skills
    182–3
personality traits 97–9, 189–93
persuasion 134
Peters, Tom 4, 155
planning 191
    contingency 129–30
    one year at a time 110
    setting milestones 143–4, 155
Pollard, John 47
portable mindset 104–7
portfolio careers 76–7, 104–7
power hunger 190
Premier Farnell 20
productivity 61–2, 86
professional indemnity insurance 129
professional restlessness 160
professionals, new 79–82

project management 33, 37–41, 110–13
Pro-tem 119

quick wins 144, 146–7

Raad voor Interim Management
    (RIM) 79
Rainmaker Inc. 35
reasons for using interim managers
    49–70
  business case 55–7
  competitive acceleration 57–9
  flexible resourcing 52–5
  interim vs company doctor 68–9
  interim vs consultant 62–5
  interim vs outsourcing 65–8
  interim vs permanent manager 60–2
  value for money 59–60
recovery 33, 41–4, 68–9, 103
recycled retirees 92
redundancy 6–7, 7–8, 73, 76, 86, 105
Regional Electricity Companies
    (RECs) 164
  see also London Electricity
relationships 110
Rent-an-MBA 119, 122
reporting lines 64, 86, 149
  clarification of 128
reputation 47, 125, 133
resourcing
  flexible 52–5
  staffing trends 6–9, 21–4
  strategic resource 23–4
restlessness, professional 160
Reynolds, Dick 137
Robinson, Peter 20
role, capability and 172–3
roles of the interim manager 27–48
  'booster rocket' role 31–3
  flexible solution 30–1
  gap management 33, 33–7
  mentoring 33, 44–6, 86, 174–6
  project management 33, 37–41,
    110–13

turnarounds 33, 41–4, 68–9, 103
Rose, Stuart 20
rules 192
Russam, Charles 73, 101
Russam GMS 101, 119

'safe pair of hands' 57, 96
Safeway 164
Sanders & Sidney 74
Schmalensee, Richard 19
Schoemakers, Irene 14
security
  financial 82, 101–2
  of payment 127–8
selection process 125–6, 147–49
self-employment 76–7
self-reliance 91
ServiceTeam Ltd 78–9
Shamrock Organization 5, 22–3
Sheward, Philip 83, 84
Silent Generation 107
Sims, David 47
skills 131–2
  most in demand 93–5
  see also attributes of interim
    managers
small and medium-sized enterprises
    (SME) 30–1
South Africa 32
specialist intermediaries see
    intermediaries
staff awareness of interim
    appointments 151–2
staffing see resourcing
Steins, Ed 32
strategic resource 23–4
styles of working 180–2
succession 151, 152
support 128

Tangaa, John 37
Temporary Executives – Business
    Turnaround Artists 102–3
temporary staff 21–2, 22–3, 24

executive temps 74–6, 95–7
Thames Water 164
Thompson, Bill 177–80
Thompson, John A. 106–7
Thorn EMI 157–9
Thorpe, David L. 39
Tipping, Jon 68
top-notch specialists 92
Townsend, Robert 85
track record 47, 125, 132
Tropitone Furniture 43–4
trouble-shooter role 33, 41–4, 68–9, 103
Tulgan, Bruce 109–10
turnarounds 33, 41–4, 68–9, 103

United Kingdom (UK) 19, 118–19
United States (US) 19, 21–2, 103, 119

Urban, Glen 19

value-adding 110
value for money 59–60, 65
virtual companies 186
virtual interims 184–7

West Berkshire Priority Care Service
    NHS Trust 82–4
Willcocks, Leslie 66–7
Wood, Martin 53, 95–6, 96–7, 97,
    120–1, 141
Woolwich Building Society 20
work ethic 191
Wright, Tony 45–6

Young, Stephen 158